I'm Not Ready for This

I'm Not Ready for This

(EVERYBODY JUST CALM DOWN AND GIVE ME A MINUTE)

Anna Lind Thomas

NELSON
BOOKS

An Imprint of Thomas Nelson

Published in Nashville, Tennessee, by Nelson Books, an imprint of Thomas Nelson. Nelson Books and Thomas Nelson are registered trademarks of HarperCollins Christian Publishing, Inc.

Thomas Nelson titles may be purchased in bulk for educational, business, fundraising, or sales promotional use. For information, please e-mail SpecialMarkets@ThomasNelson.com.

Any internet addresses, phone numbers, or company or product information printed in this book are offered as a resource and are not intended in any way to be or to imply an endorsement by Thomas Nelson, nor does Thomas Nelson vouch for the existence, content, or services of these sites, phone numbers, companies, or products beyond the life of this book.

ISBN 978-1-4002-2208-7 (audiobook)
ISBN 978-1-4002-2207-0 (eBook)
ISBN 978-1-4002-2201-8 (TP)

Library of Congress Control Number: 2022932782

Printed in the United States of America
22 23 24 25 26 LSC 10 9 8 7 6 5 4 3 2 1

To Dad.
The two of us, always laughing.
Thick as thieves, you and me.

Contents

Introduction

When I was writing my master's thesis, I got into an explosive fight with my thesis chair. That may seem odd, the thought of a student and professor, in a professional setting, going at it over how to measure cognitive dissonance. But there we were, like a couple of unhinged weirdos. I burst into tears unexpectedly, then quickly tried to reel myself in. My tears laid my vulnerability bare, and my professor's shoulders slowly lowered from her ears. She softened, and we reconciled. When it was time to leave, she gave me a hug, and as I leaned in, the unspeakable happened. For reasons I'll never understand, I whispered softly in her ear, "I love you."

The very second it left my lips I knew I had no choice but to drop out of school, glue on a beard, move to a quiet town, and hide under an ambiguous name like Pat Stephens. I mean, was I nuts? I respected her, sure, but she could be a real piece of work. Brilliant, unrelenting in her demands for excellence, and terrifying for no good reason. To say I loved her was a real stretch. The cringe ran so deep and hard, it kinked my neck and my limbs froze to ice.

She said nothing in return, just patted my back politely,

and then watched me leave her office, my neck kinked at a 90-degree angle, limping, rigid, like an ice sculpture.

To say I wasn't ready to return to class the next day is an understatement. How could I look her in the eye again? But I somehow managed, detached and bubbly as if that erased the cringe from existence. It worked well enough, I guess. With her guidance, I eventually went on to write a thesis worthy of awards.

Now that I think of it, I've never been ready for anything. I've tried to recall a time when I've walked into any situation prepared academically, emotionally, spiritually, or physically. Nothing comes to mind. Adult decisions, marriage, conflict, parenting, crow's-feet, large pores, skinny jeans, hosting a dinner party . . . you name it, I'm not ready for it.

I've never, not once, been ready to go sleeveless. Or for my monthly period to arrive, even though my iWatch gives me several warnings. I wasn't ready for my daughter to start kindergarten, and don't even get me started on that one time I appeared on national TV in a blazer two sizes too small because I thought I'd lose 20 pounds before the shoot. Oh Lord, I ain't never ready!

But somehow, miraculously, God finds a way to push me forward. Feels super rude, to be honest, as I kick and scream, weep, and breathe into a paper sack. But the more I'm pushed, the more I've had to rely on God for a miracle. A reminder that I can accomplish anything I set my mind to while simultaneously recognizing I can't accomplish anything at all.

Every huge moment of my life, something has given me a push. In fact, I probably wouldn't be alive today if I wasn't, literally, violently pushed. It's a sliver of time in my life I think of often. A reminder, or a metaphor maybe. There is something pushing us forward all the time, and it's wise to let it happen.

I don't remember many of the details, other than the shock of it and the chaos swirling around me. The screaming and running, the confusion and fear. I can still see my mom running toward me. I was surprised to see her; I usually walked home with my friends. Her eyes looked afraid. It was just one tiny second, but I thought maybe she was running to hug me. But she pushed me, hard, and I flew back several feet. Skidding across the gravel, my elbows skinned raw. The picture I had painted at school, the one I held in my hands, caught the air like a paper sack, flipping and twirling above me. I heard screams, saw people running. My classmate's mother, Jody, scooped me into her arms and carried me away. I don't remember anything else.

But my mom remembers it vividly. And thirty-four years later, she says, she's still in shock it ever happened.

I was in the first grade. We lived in the country, outside of a small Nebraska town. I attended Stull School, a tiny three-room schoolhouse. It's hard to imagine tiny schoolhouses still standing today. A few years ago, I drove by my beautiful old home on the hill. I was disappointed to see Stull converted into a day care center. The playground was now gated, and the building looked shabby and sad. Cheap, beat-up toys were strewn across what looked like a prison yard. The same stretch of grass where I used to run free with my friends.

The day started just like any other day. Mom helped me

get dressed, comb my hair, and brush my teeth. I had a little breakfast, and when it was time, she helped me tie my shoes and wrap my backpack across my shoulders. I would walk to school with my friend and her older sister, so I waited at the front door for them to appear into view. After a few moments, I saw them outside my house on the gravel road, pausing to see if I'd join them. I yelled goodbye and ran out to meet them; Mom waved me off at the front door.

But what made this day peculiar is what happened later in the afternoon. On a typical school day, I would walk home with those same friends, and about a half hour before-hand, Mom would prepare a little snack for when I walked through the door. But on this day, while she began to rustle up ingredients, she was struck with an immediate sense of urgency. It wasn't a gentle, inner knowing. Not a little nudge, or whisper in her ear. It was an inner bullhorn: I was in danger, and she needed to run.

If you were to ask her what it felt like, the only word she can conjure is *robotic*. As if something, or someone, had taken over her body, and she was left to observe, con-fused and concerned. As someone else grabbed her keys. As someone else started the car. As someone else pushed the accelerator, down, then up, then down the gravel road to the tiny three-room schoolhouse where children trickled from its doors.

She spotted me immediately, holding the picture I painted for her that day, making my way home. Mom felt pushed from her car, not given the chance to shut off the engine or close the driver's-side door. She ran toward me, across the street, as a large dump truck gunned it in reverse.

That's when I saw her. I lit up, until I saw her eyes. She was afraid, but why? Then she pushed me. I remember the pain and a feeling of betrayal. Then a woman scooped me into her arms and ran toward the school so I wouldn't witness the truck crash into my mom, knock her to the ground, and roll over her entire body.

That particular road had been padded with fresh gravel just a week before, and my mom sunk into it, deep. Then came more screams, the arms waving at the man to stop his truck. Others ran to her to see how badly she was hurt. She tells me that bruises immediately appeared, dark and blue, from her neck down to her ankles. Without a single broken bone.

When I hear this story I like to think of Acts 12:7, when Peter is asleep in a jail cell and an angel hits him on the side. Startled, Peter wakes up and sees his shackles are open. "Quick!" the angel says. "Get up!"

Peter thought he was in a dream, but he couldn't help but do what he was told.

Last week, as my mom and I revisited the story over the phone, she said, "You know what the driver did after he realized he ran over me? He blamed me! Said I was stupid for standing behind a moving truck."

"Typical," I said, rolling my eyes. *The nerve of that idiot.* For a moment so extraordinary, a miracle beyond human understanding, man somehow remains predictable. Distracted. So self-involved.

But mercifully, we're still granted those rare magical moments when something, or someone, gives us a little push. Of course, we're never ready. But maybe that's the point.

CHAPTER 1
Only God Is Perfect

One year ago, to this day, I sat on a curb, crying out in shock and horror. I grew up in the '80s, so it was easy to channel my best Nancy Kerrigan, the real-life scene when the poor girl got clubbed in the knee. But instead of wearing a shimmering ice-skating ensemble, surrounded by adoring fans and cameras, I was wearing sweatpants and a ribbed tank top all alone in an empty parking lot. Well, I wasn't completely alone; my mom was there. And no one clubbed me in the knee, per se, I just wasn't paying attention and rolled my ankle off a curb. "*Why?*" I shouted, mouth agape, tears on the cusp of pouring down my cheeks. "Not now! This can't be happening now! Why, Mom, *why?*"

Mom joined me as if we were in a musical. "Oh, not now, Anna! Not now! Who's gonna drive the car? Anna! *Why?*"

Our chorus of screams and intense shock and despair were on par with seeing someone fall off a cliff. I mean, I rolled my ankle off a curb. Can we dust ourselves off and move forward?

We drove together from Omaha, Nebraska, to Chico, California, in my cute little Volkswagen Passat. After graduating from the University of Nebraska–Lincoln and spending many of those years as a resident assistant (RA), I was hired at Chico State University as an assistant residence coordinator. I'd grown from RA to boss of the RAs and felt quite pleased with myself. Mom helped me move into my on-campus apartment, and the two of us were feeling jazzy. I was just starting my next great adventure, and Mom desperately needed a change of scenery. My Passat was a stick shift, so I drove the entire way while Mom was in charge of handing me snacks and rewinding the book on tape we were listening to. "Wait, Kim murdered James?" I'd interrupt, flicking the cassette on pause. "When? Where was I?"

"Haven't you been listening for the past three hours?" she'd say, losing her patience. This was the fourth time she had to rewind the book because I was daydreaming, missing huge plot points.

Now I was sitting on a curb in total despair. "If only we hadn't taken the trash out, none of this would've happened," Mom lamented, rubbing my back, cursing our misfortune.

"I know," I said, quietly, weeping. "I know."

Things had been going way too smooth, and we were way too happy. Of course one of us would crack an ankle! Just moments before, we were zipping around, possessed with good feelings. Blame our excitement on the buzz of new beginnings in northern California, but we were zingy, busy, cleaning, prepping, buying, organizing, and loving life. At one point, Mom stopped to make us a salad, seasoned with olive oil, vinegar, and salt and pepper. She handed me a plate, and honestly, our reaction to it was a bit much. "I'm sorry, but this is literally the best salad I've ever tasted," I said, shoveling in heaping forkfuls of spring lettuce. "Is it the California produce? Is that what's making the difference?" she replied, dead serious. "These flavors are stunning!" I mean, it's not like we cut the lettuce from a garden, ripened under the California sun. We bought it at Safeway, the same stuff from Mexico that gets shipped to Omaha. But I suppose everything looks better, tastes better, and smells better when a page to an exciting new chapter has turned.

We had a lot of boxes and trash from the move, so we took a trip out to the bins. It was then, with a huge garbage bag in my arms, that I stepped off the curb and instantly twisted my ankle in the same place I had twisted it years before. I wasn't so much surprised as I was devastatingly inconvenienced. We'd been so excited, embarking on a new adventure together, navigating a new city, making Target runs, and assembling new furniture, that we couldn't handle a single wrench in our joy, especially a wrench that limited my mobility.

Although I wanted to make a good first impression with my new bosses and coworkers, I had no choice but to hobble into the conference room for our first staff meeting. I tried to hide the limp, but doing so made my movements rigid and pronounced, as if I were doing the robot at a club. "I rolled my ankle a couple of days ago," I had to explain to my new coworkers watching me with confusion and compassion in their eyes. "It's nothing, really." True, my left leg looked normal, with proper curvature, ankle bones, and so on, and my right leg looked like a bursting tube of sausage, but this wasn't the kind of first impression I had hoped to make. For the next two weeks, I'd walk around campus as if my hip had been replaced, but it eventually healed. Again.

Ready to roll on a dime.

My ankle has been a slippery little wuss ever since college. I'd like to tell you I was an athlete injured while giving it my all on the field or court or whatever, but I'm afraid I was just running, no faster than a brisk walk, because I had completely forgotten I had to work that night and was already fifteen minutes late. I was on duty and running toward my dorm, Smith Hall. I wasn't a nimble, agile young lady. My running included violent boob slaps and an overall jostling that proved I was just barely in control. I was on campus studying when an uptight RA named Irene called my phone. She was the type who would take great pleasure in seeing me written up "because it's only fair," so I really gave it my all as I made my way back to the dorm. As I neared the entrance, I heard someone call out my name, and as I turned, I landed my step right on the side of my foot, snapping my ankle violently in on itself.

Experiencing an accidental injury in public shouldn't be embarrassing, but I find it utterly humiliating. I suppose athletes experience more despair, but that's because they're in the midst of competition. They're a casualty on the battlefield, and the consequences are dire. But I was just an unfit young woman, wearing a Nebraska hoodie and sweatpants, running as if she smuggled an iMac under her shirt and was getting chased by Best Buy's management. I knew immediately by all the snap, crackle sounds that the sprain was bad. Kristin, the one who called out my name, ran to my aid.

"Yeeesh, are you okay?" she asked. Dumb question, because my embarrassment over public falls, even dire ones, will never allow me to admit I'm seriously injured. If I were, say, walking down a bustling city street and managed to trip, fall, and impale myself on a sharp pole, I'd still play it off like it never even happened. "No, no, no. Oh, you're too kind! Don't be silly. I'm fine, really. Just a little blood, nothing I can't manage. Say, could you all walk away? I need to make a quick phone call. No, not 911! Oh, you're too cute. I just, um, have to check in with my boss, and we're going over some confidential figures. Quickly now, walk away. *That means you, lady! Now!* Thanks so much."

Dramatic, hilarious, mortifying falls appear to be a genetic trait because my father also biffs it on a regular basis. He's had some embarrassing falls, and I don't even want to talk about it because I still get the chill of humiliation by simple proxy. He holds our good family name; he can't be falling around all over town! He's a luxury homebuilder in our community, a leader, a man with dignity and respect. And when he falls in public like Chris Farley in a *Saturday Night Live* skit, yes, I laugh because it's impossible not to, but I also get a red, hot stress rash on my chest.

A few years ago, he was checking on one of his homes when he stepped on a nail barely sticking out of a two-by-four. It got stuck in the heel of his boot and caused him to literally dive headfirst into a huge pile of Styrofoam. A drywall crew was eating lunch nearby and witnessed the whole thing. Only a few of them spoke English, but their shouts of concern and empathetic embarrassment were universally understood. The boss of the crew spoke up, "Oh, Mister Lind! Are you okay? Oh my, my, my, that looked bad." Who among us can command respect after tripping and falling into a huge pile of trash?

Another time he was touring a house with a buyer and their real estate agent. As they made their way down the stairs, Dad's front shoe slid to the next step. He was unable to correct it without making a fuss, so he made the unspeakable calculation to just go with it, as he ever so slowly did the splits. To make matters worse, he kept sliding, his back leg straight behind him, but no one was brave enough to call attention to it. "So, how many bedrooms are on the lower level?" the buyer asked, now looking down at my dad as he white-knuckled the handrail. "Two," Dad replied, still sliding, thumping every time he hit a new step, "but one of them would make a perfect office space."

When I was in my early twenties, my family got together at a local park. We had a picnic spread in a large, cemented gazebo area, and my dad bought a pogo stick for the grandkids to have something fun to do. The older kids tried it out but couldn't get the hang of it. "Here, I'll show you," he said, popping a chip in his mouth before getting on. "I used to pogo all over town when I was a kid." I sat back and watched my dad bounce, impressed by how easily it came back to him. But over time, I noticed his bounces were getting higher and higher and instead of remaining in one place, he started to bounce around in a large circle, getting precariously close to some of the smaller, more vulnerable grandchildren. His expression went from playful, to concerned, to terrified. It didn't take long for his bounces to become life threatening. "Dad," I shouted over the rhythmic squeaking of the pogo stick, "shouldn't you be wearing a helmet?" But he wasn't listening, his predicament demanded focus. Then my sister, growing increasingly agitated, called out, "Dad, can you stop? This is dangerous!" And at that, he took two huge bounces, covering at least four feet at each bounce, before launching himself over a couple of picnic tables. He landed out of sight as the entire family gasped in unison, running around the tables like a school of fish. *Oh Lord, please don't let him break a hip*, I thought. My brother belted out, "Dad, are you dead?" We weren't sure where his body was exactly, so when he popped up and said, "Ta-da!" he startled us, making us gasp and lean back. "Well, is anything broken?" Mom hissed. He was in his fifties! Absolutely ridiculous.

But that's the weird thing—nothing ever breaks on this man. While his homes or buildings were under construction, he's fallen through holes straight from the top floor to the basement. He's fallen off the beds of trucks. He's fallen down flights of stairs. And he's flown off pogo sticks. He usually gets a nasty bruise and a bit of a limp, but that's it. Say what you want about boomers—they're tough as nails.

I longed for my dad's ability to seamlessly bounce back from a humiliating fall, but my injury felt too ominous. While my lower lip vibrated like a plucked guitar string, I ignored Kristin's questions about how I was doing and crawled around for my books, dragging my ankle behind me. Kristin was in nursing school, and her limited training kicked in right away. She helped me up, I put my arm around her shoulders, and I walked gingerly into the building. I had a Pier 1 Imports papasan chair, a staple in every early 2000s dorm room, where she helped sit me down. "We need to get a cold compress on it," she said, before running up to her room to retrieve one. She quickly returned. "Sorry, couldn't find one, but I have this."

"You have frozen okra in your minifridge?" I asked.

"Long story," she said, stacking my schoolbooks on a nearby chair, placing a pillow on top, then dragging it over to the papasan so I could elevate my foot. Sure, this was Nursing 101, but Kristin moved with conviction, as if she were born for this.

The on-campus doctor looked it over the next day and diagnosed it as a high ankle sprain. Elevation, ice, and time were pretty much all I could do. After he left the room, I was left unsatisfied by his treatment plan. An injured athlete gets their own athletic trainer, and I get thrown into the streets to hobble on my own? How could I manage around campus? I secretly hoped Kristin could take a week off school to help tend to me with her frozen okra and stack of books. College thrust me into independence, and it was so exciting, it took hobbling across campus on crutches to realize how precious a caretaker can be. But I didn't want to be a bother, hoping to prove to myself I could handle it. And I did, slowly—grimacing and cursing how hard it is to get your hands on some frozen vegetables in a residence hall.

A dark bruise had formed about two inches above my ankle and over time the blood dropped, making most of my foot a deep black color, as if it were dead and decomposing. For the next few weeks, my ankle couldn't take much pressure, so I'd lift it while standing, like a dog with a thorn in her paw. In the next month or so, it would heal completely, but my ankle would never be the same. Twisting and turning and slipping and gliding over nothing, really. At the most inconvenient of times.

I wouldn't say I'm codependent with my mom, but if she doesn't answer my phone call, there will be hell to pay. Just the other day, I wanted to discuss the chicken salad sandwich I ate, but she didn't answer when I called. No need to panic. I figured a quick follow-up text would allow her a few more moments to finish running to her phone. After twenty agonizing minutes, I called my dad to make sure he wasn't with her in the emergency room or something. When he didn't pick up, I had no choice but to file a missing person report. As the officer jotted down my information, Mom's text came in. "Ope, there she is," I told him. "Never mind." I hung up on him midsentence and pulled up the text. "Sorry honey," it read. "Out with my sisters, call later." I tossed my phone down in disgust. Does that woman think of anyone other than herself?

Maybe it's not right, but I feel deeply entitled to her time. Besides, I do my best to make it worth her while. Throughout the years, I've persuaded her to join me on various adventures and to be my round-the-clock counselor as I navigate my writing career. A brilliant writer in her own right, she reads and edits my work first so I don't embarrass myself. I can only assume when I insist she abandon her cart at the grocery store to speed home and read my work, it's the greatest joy of her life.

When my first book, *We'll Laugh About This Someday*, was in its final pass and I needed to read through it once more before it went to print, Mom wanted to read it again as well. I decided to print two copies for us at a FedEx Kinko's for a better reading experience and wanted to upgrade to the good paper because I'm worth it. But that made it real pricey, so I decided I'd just get one luxurious copy for my mom to enjoy.

She was spending the Saturday with me when I stopped to pick up the printout. As I was leaving with my box, I noticed my petite mother looked like a hobbit in the front seat of my car, and it gave me a bad case of the giggles. Her little head would pop up, look around, then disappear from view. Her head would suddenly appear again, looking around like a little prairie dog, before disappearing out of sight.

What is she doing? I thought to myself. She was really making me laugh, and I was in the middle of a deep chuckle when, as if in a recurring nightmare, I took a step and instantly snapped my ankle on the curb. I heard it crinkle and pop four times on my way down to my other knee, skidding it against the pavement. To catch myself, I had to do the unthinkable—I threw my box in the air. All three hundred pages of my book flew into the sky like three hundred white doves. Flipping and spinning and lighter than air. The wind picked up, and the pages of my book flew, in an almost beautiful, meditative way. I looked up hoping Mom had witnessed what just happened and would help me, but naturally the little prairie dog was nowhere to be found.

"Mom! *Mom!*" I was on my hands and one nonbloody knee, trying to scoop up papers as they flew around. "Seriously? *Mooooom!*" As I screamed the final "Mom!" she heard me, saw me, and scrambled from the car.

"Oh, Anna! Oh no no no no *noooooooooo!*" She fluttered around the parking lot, chasing down papers, several landing and splashing in puddles. "Oh, how did this happen to us again! *Why?*" she screamed about the parking lot, chasing, flapping.

"I don't even *knoooooooooow,*" I wailed against the wind.

I nestled into my familiar Nancy Kerrigan position, cradling my ankle for the third time. It appears my nemesis isn't Tonya Harding, but curbs. There were people around this time, so I was too embarrassed to really lean into loud self-pity. I tried to look casual, there on the curb, blood beginning to ooze from my knee, scraped raw, mouthing "*Why?*" quietly.

I even paid extra for the good paper.

A Good Samaritan joined my mom, chasing down all

three hundred papers, and watching them chase the paper like they were chasing chickens made me want to throw in the towel. "It's not worth it, just throw it in the trash, guys!" I said, trying to get up. "Really, let's just throw what we caught away, please stop worrying!" I winced as I watched my pricey paper fly in the air, some in puddles, others getting driven over by people who I could tell felt awful for my plight but didn't have time to get involved.

I got up, dragging my leg behind me, as blood dripped down my other leg. "Let's call it, guys, really. This isn't the original copy of the Bible, it's fine." *I mean, can we stop? My ankle's swelling and needs to get on ice!*

But Mom and the Good Samaritan refused to be detoured from their mission. "Mom, that's enough, let's just get in the car," I barked. My ankle was beginning to smart, and so was I.

"Oh, Anna! How could this happen? Let's go inside and see if they'll print us another for free."

"No, it's not worth it, it's fine."

"I bet she saw you fall! Surely she'd print out another for free."

The visual of the woman watching me exit the store as I suddenly disappear in a puff of paper smoke was compelling, but I didn't need her pity. There was absolutely no way I was going to hobble back in, now filthy, dripping with blood, and dragging my rapidly swelling ankle behind me to go beg. "*Hiiiiiii,*" I'd say, long and drawn out, looking like I'd fallen into a sewer. "Not sure if you saw what happened out there, but could you give me another print free of charge?" Nope, not happening—she could keep the forty dollars.

"Mom, just get in the car!"

But no one would listen to me, and eventually Mom and the Good Samaritan were able to get every last one of the three hundred pages. "I'll dry these out at home. They'll be good as new," she told me.

"Mom, give it up! There are dirty leaves stuck all over them," I protested.

She slowly thumbed through the stack and said gently, "It's a reminder that only God is perfect."

And I guess I couldn't argue with that. We thanked the man, and I hobbled back into the driver's seat. Mom sat beside me, the wet, dirty pages of my new book sitting in her lap.

"Remember when you rolled your ankle in California?" she asked, giggling to herself.

"Why God, why?" I said, mimicking my previous self.

"Who's gonna drive the car now?" Mom added.

We laughed to ourselves for a long while until gently trailing off.

"I paid extra for the good paper," I said quietly.

"I know, sweetheart," Mom said, touching my arm. "But I'm sure you'll find a way to put this in your next book."

CHAPTER 2
Heefy-Jeebies

I was nervous getting out of the car, the idea of just walking into their house had me on edge. I'm not proud of it, but I wanted to leave the ham and mashed potatoes on their stoop and burn rubber. I'm no good at grief, particularly if it isn't my own. I don't know what to do or say. I don't know what to look at, how long to hug, or what to do with my facial expressions. And it's not even supposed to be about

15

me, but me is the only thing I can think about. Am I saying the right thing? Showing affection in the right way? Is my face compassionate, understanding, and warm, or contorted as if I have a urinary tract infection? It turns me into a hot mess I'd prefer to avoid.

This was just further proof I am my father's daughter. Swedish, cool, and impersonal. Not because I don't feel emotions, but because it's too awkward, painful, or irrational to express them outside of my home. And yet, I'm also my mother's daughter. Sicilian—passionate and loving. Unafraid to throw a cast-iron skillet at someone's head if they deserve it. The Swedish and Sicilian intertwine inside me somehow, evoked at different times, depending on context and mood. But as I've gotten older and my relationship with God has grown deeper, his deep love and compassion for me has chiseled away at my more selfish edges. And somehow, unexpectedly, I've developed the desire to do the right thing, even if I don't want to.

Besides, I couldn't really drop the food off and run because my mom was in the car with me. The hot cross buns she made late into the night were sitting on her lap, waiting to impress. At the very least, she deserved the satisfaction of seeing someone eat one of her buns; she was glazing well past midnight!

We were sitting in the driveway, the car running, both of us quiet and contemplative, when I broke the silence. "So, what are we going to see exactly? Do they have him set up in a bed? Is he awake and aware of what's going on?"

"I don't know, honey. They didn't give me details," Mom said somberly. She looked on past the house. "He really is

16

my favorite." Out of all my dad's brothers and sisters, she and my dad had the closest relationship with Hank and his wife, Beth. They would go out to dinner and laugh all night, recounting stories of their childhood. Whenever I see my uncle, I marvel at how much he looks like my own father. Maybe that's why, in some strange way, he's my favorite too.

"Do you think we should even see him if he's that way? Maybe we should just drop the food off, say our hellos, and leave them to grieve."

"Let's just go in and take our cues from the family."

It felt wrong somehow, to walk in with a ham and soft biscotti cookies, to stand bedside and watch Uncle Hank die before my eyes. It felt unearned, vulgar even. Although my dad had a good relationship with his baby brother, I wasn't very close to my uncle. I loved him in the way you love a fun relative who dressed up as Santa at family reunions, but we didn't have a personal relationship. Who was I to any of them, really?

It was two days before Easter when his daughter, Chelsea, texted me to let me know that her dad was discharged from the hospital for at-home hospice care, and there was little time left. She said my mom wasn't answering her phone and asked if I'd pass it along. I knew Uncle Hank had throat cancer years ago, but his treatment, while taking his voice, didn't take his life, and I thought things were okay. On the car ride to his house, Mom shared that every so often, his throat would begin to close, and they would have to take him in to have it stretched so he could continue to eat, breathe, and live. But they knew this couldn't last forever. That at some point, his throat wouldn't stretch anymore.

17

And, two days before Easter, the day had come. His throat ripped, and nothing more could be done. They gave him the option to spend his final moments at home, with detailed instructions on what to do when his throat closed for the final time.

"Can't they do *something?*" I wondered out loud. "Put a hole in his throat and hook it to some contraption so he can breathe? Be fed through a tube?"

"I think they would have considered that if it was an option," Mom said.

We got out of the car, and I opened the trunk. I baked ham and made mashed potatoes along with my famous southern baked beans. Mom had made our family's soft biscotti and hot cross buns. After my text from Chelsea, I worried they would be in such grief over Easter weekend, they wouldn't have any food at home during the holiday.

"Should we make them an Easter dinner?" I asked my mom over the phone.

"I didn't even think of that," she said. "Yes, let's do. I'll make them hot cross buns and biscotti. Pick me up so we can drop it off together."

When we got off the phone, I pulled out a piece of paper to start jotting down my grocery list, but as my list grew, so did my doubts. This was going to be a bit of an expense, mostly in time, but a big ole ham ain't cheap either. What if they don't need it? What if they aren't home? What if we stop by and they're all sitting by his bed chomping on a pepperoni pizza? I called my mom to share my concerns.

"Why don't you text Chelsea and ask her?" she said.

"I could, but don't grieving people tend to decline when asked? I remember reading an article on *HuffPost* about this." I tried googling the article. "Like, I remember you shouldn't say, 'Please let me know if there's anything I can do,' because that puts the ball in their court, and they're too overwhelmed. And if you ask if you can bring them food, they'll say no for the same reason."

"Well, what did the article say we're supposed to do then?" she asked. Her tone read like she was just as clueless as I was, and honestly, it bothered me a little.

"Well, don't you know? I would think this is something you learn by the time you get to be your age."

"You'd think, but I have no idea," she snapped. "What did the article say?"

I couldn't remember, but I did have a friend who'd know what to do. Danelle is the type of person who will fly across the country to attend the funeral of her estranged cousin's third wife simply because it's the right thing to do. She lives by those standards, while I usually play it fast and loose and google things like "What should I do?" and then do nothing. I hung up on Mom and called her.

"Well, funny you should ask," Danelle said. "We just had a training on this at work."

I knew I'd called the right person. "Go on. . . ." I leaned in, all ears.

"People who are grieving don't want to be forced into making decisions, and they say no most of the time because it's the easiest answer. The best thing to do is to simply state your intentions, don't ask them permission." I furiously scribbled notes. "Just tell your cousin that you're stopping by to drop off some food at a particular time, and you want to make sure someone will be home to receive it. Don't give her options, or it will only add to their stress."

"Uh-huh. Okay."

"And, you know, if they specifically ask you not to after that, or whatever, then of course, don't force your food on them. Be cool about it."

"Be . . . cool . . . about . . . it," I scribbled. "Got it." I slapped my pen down. "Danelle, you're a national treasure!" and then I hung up on her without saying goodbye.

I pulled up my messages and texted Chelsea.

> Hi there. My mom and I will be dropping food off tomorrow at 11. We'll just drop it off, we don't want to be a bother. It should be enough to feed the whole crew. We won't stay long, we don't want to be a bother. Please let me know if you'd prefer another time.

I hit send, read over my text, and had immediate regrets by my nervous repetition of "we won't be a bother." I sighed, annoyed. *Nothing I can do about it now.*

Within seconds she wrote back.

"That time works great. Thank you so much."

It worked! I was quite pleased with myself. I wanted to do something good and had permission to do it. "Looks like we're gonna be up late cooking," I told Mom over the phone.

"Alright then," she said. "I better get going or I'll be up all night."

Mom and I stepped into the open door, balancing the food in our arms. "Hello?" Mom called out into the home. My aunt Beth appeared at the top of the staircase.

"Oh, hi! Come on in!" she said, welcoming us with enthusiasm.

I don't know what I was expecting while walking into their home, but upbeat pleasantries weren't it. I suppose I assumed it would be more like walking into a quiet funeral parlor where no one's manning the front desk. Her enthusiasm confused me, and I grew suspicious. I shifted only my eyes, tentative with each step, unprepared to see a man near death. I envisioned him in bed, partially conscious, tubes or ventilators or other life-sustaining contraptions connected all over him. The thought of it made my feet heavy, my cadence melancholy. I didn't feel brave enough to see it, even if it meant I'd never see him again.

We walked up the stairs, and Aunt Beth invited us into the kitchen to put our food down. I turned the corner into the kitchen, and stopped so fast, Mom ran into the back of me. "Well, hi, Uncle Hank!" I shouted, startling even myself. He was sitting at the kitchen table looking healthy and rather handsome, laughing with Chelsea's husband and their children (albeit making no sound). A bottle of Corona sat upside down in his feeding bag.

You know, this was a thirty-dollar ham, I thought to myself. *Does hospice not mean what I think it means?* Mom and I made eyes before I blurted, "You're looking so good!"

"Hi, hi, hi," he said in a raspy whisper. He rose from the table as we came in and set our food down. He pointed at the beer that was upside down in the pocket of a feeding bag. "My friend is coming over soon," he whispered. "We usually have a beer together; it's just a little joke."

"Yeah, all the wires are from my iPhone cords," Chelsea added, pulling the beer out to show how the wires were taped on with masking tape.

"And we've got a sense of humor!" I said, lining up the food on the counter. I turned, my eyes narrowed as if I were Sherlock Holmes trying to deduce what was really going on here. "I like your slippers" was all I could think to say. He was wearing a black V-neck T-shirt with comfortable black pants and attractive camel-colored slippers. "How come Dad never dresses comfortable and handsome like this?" I asked my mom.

"I've tried," she sighed. "He won't even wear shorts. He's got great legs too. It's a shame."

Dad is a little bizarre when it comes to clothes, although I've grown up with it my whole life, so I tend to stop seeing it until someone else mentions it. When Rob and I were first married and visiting my parents, he leaned in and asked, "Does your dad not own shorts and a T-shirt?" The answer is no. He wears Ralph Lauren button-up shirts with jeans every single day, and he wears them the moment he wakes up until he goes to bed. He wears that combo in the dead heat of summer, at the pool, at Disney World, and I think he wears it exercising. It was so refreshing to see a man who looks just like my dad be a little casual and relaxed for a change!

But soon after complimenting his slippers, I couldn't find any more words. My brain offered me various options, all of them completely inappropriate. *Try this*, my brain said.

"I think the real tragedy here is that you can't eat my baked beans."

Are you nuts? I told myself. Poor taste.

Okay, okay, I'm just riffing here. Alright, how's this? Take a bite of the mashed potatoes and say, "The good news is that God's a much better cook." Eh, eh? Come on, you know that's good!

I don't like admitting it, but I laughed a little on that one. Yeah, that's good, but it's also sickening. Just calm down and see if Mom will pick up the slack.

Fortunately, I didn't need to rely on Mom's small talk skills because Uncle Hank's friend arrived with a six-pack of beer, our cue it was a good time to leave.

"We'll leave you to visit with your friend," I said, opening my arms for a hug. Uncle Hank stood and hugged me. He seemed extremely tall for some reason, and I wondered if he'd always been that tall and why I never noticed. "I love you," I said.

"I love you too," he whispered, raspy and soft. As Mom went in to hug him, I pulled away, allowing her to say to him the things she wanted to say, in private. I backed up out of the kitchen and watched him smile at whatever it was my mom was saying, trying to cement the image of him in my mind. No, I'd never really been close to him, but I didn't want to forget him either.

Aunt Beth met us at the staircase to see us out, and she seemed to guess at what we were thinking.

"He looks good, but the hospice nurse warned us about false hope," she said. "When his throat closes, and it will soon, that will be the end." I examined her eyes, her mannerisms, to see how she was really feeling. On the surface she seemed her normal self, but if you looked closely, right behind the eyes, you could tell she was operating on a detached level of consciousness. Fueled by adrenaline, you could almost hear the rapid heartbeat in her voice. Her brain offering her words to say, but her soul in hiding until it was over. "And I have so much to do," she went on. "I have to call Heefy, Heefy, and Heefy still, and I just really don't want to."

I chuckled a little when she said Heefy, Heefy, and Heefy, and I noticed Mom's lip curl upward too. It's a mortuary, and every time I drive by that place, the name drives me nuts. Can't you just call it Heefy Mortuary? Like, we need to know three individual Heefys created this place? The people are grieving, just give us the gist!

"That place gives me the Heefy-jeebies," I threw out unexpectedly. It poured out so fast, I even surprised myself. The worst part was I started laughing at my own joke. Mom heard it too and dipped into her abyss laugh, the kind that spirals down so deep, she can't stop until she's lost all her eye makeup, peed her pants, and needs to remove herself from public spaces. She grabbed my arm tight, partly to settle herself, but also to signal to me that we can't fall in. It was inappropriate, and we must pull out immediately and gain our composure. Aunt Beth didn't catch my joke but also didn't seem too troubled by our laughing. In fact, she didn't seem to notice at all.

"He's been so busy and active around the house, replacing our light fixtures and painting the walls," she continued. "He just wants to get as much done around the house as he can, you know, before he goes."

"You know," I said, clearing my throat, "they say that

men who have a job to do live longer. Just give him a huge honey-do list and keep adding to it," I said. "Put 'Replace the roof' on it. That'll really keep him busy." I meant that comment in light humor, to help ease her tension, but the idea wasn't half bad.

Aunt Beth laughed and acknowledged the idea had some merit. "We've known this was coming for a long time, but this is too much for one person. I'm responsible for his final moments, you know. He'll be struggling and gasping, and the nurse said I'll be tempted to call 911," she paused, her lips pressed tight. "But the paramedics are required to try and save him, so I can't do that. I'm supposed to call her, and then give him a pill that will stop his brain from panicking so he can die peacefully. I just, I mean, who wants to be responsible for this?" Aunt Beth blinked repetitively, her eyes growing glassier each time. She took a breath as if to keep talking but couldn't find the words.

"Let me hug you," my mom said opening her arms. "You don't have to talk, let me just hold you for a little while." I stepped away while they held each other tight. Chelsea was behind me, so I turned to her to give them privacy. We made small talk the best we could, and eventually we discussed our elderly dogs. She recommended an arthritic chew she gives hers that really seemed to help. The topic helped us waste some time, distracting us from her dad laughing in the kitchen but dying any minute.

On the way home, I noticed I smelled like Uncle Hank's cologne. "Thank you for thinking to do this," Mom said. "I don't know why, but it never crossed my mind to bring them food. I'm so glad I got to see him."

"I'm glad we did this too," I said. "Think they'll like the beans?"

She looked out the passenger side window for a long while. "He really is my favorite."

<hr />

Right as I laid my head on the pillow, I heard thunder. "Oh là là," I said to Rob. "I didn't know it was going to storm tonight." Falling asleep to the delightful sounds of rain and thunder is my jam.

"I didn't either," Rob said, pulling up his phone. "Looks kinda stormy, and it might hail," he said. "I'm gonna put the car in the garage."

I laid back, enjoying the gentle sounds of thunder, until it picked up and sounded rough. In our backyard are two gigantic oak trees that partially cover the roof of our home. I could hear several loud thumps hitting our roof, then what sounded like a freight train coming toward our home.

Rob came back into our room. "It's crazy windy," he said, crawling back into bed. We heard another branch hit our roof, shaking our bedroom. "It's a small one that sounds loud," he said, one step ahead of his wife, knowing I was going to ask if the roof was about to collapse on my face.

I tried to settle in and relax, but this was far more than a typical thunderstorm. This was "peel a roof off" kind of weather. "Am I being dramatic if I think we all need to go into the basement?" I asked him.

"Yes," he said. "It's fine." Then off somewhere in the distance, we could hear a slight whine of a siren.

"That's the tornado siren," I said.

"Okay, yep. Let's go." We jumped out of bed and walked swiftly to the girls' room.

"Girls, wake up," I said, pulling down their covers. "Grab your pillows, come on, we're going downstairs." Rob swept Poppy up into his arms.

"Okay, Mommy," Lucy said, rolling over.

"Baby, now. Let's go." I lifted her out of bed and grabbed her hand, leading her out of their room. As we all shuffled single file down the hallway, the house shuddered around us until becoming perfectly still. The lights went out, the ceiling fans slowly spun to a stop, and we stood in complete darkness. Without the gentle hum of electricity, the moving parts of air-conditioning and fans, we could hear the violent winds outside our home with even more clarity. Rob moved into the kitchen to grab a flashlight, and we all hustled down the stairs.

We have a large couch in our basement, with a chaise on each side, big enough to sleep all of us. I covered the girls in blankets and cozied up beside them. "There's no tornado warning," Rob said. "Just a severe thunderstorm. We should be okay sleeping here."

Our basement is almost entirely underground. It was so dark, I couldn't tell if my eyes were open or closed. There was also no sound. *Strange*, I thought. Had we been downstairs instead of in our beds, we'd be fast asleep, unaware a hurricane was devastating the world outside.

By morning, I was sorely disappointed while peeing in complete darkness. I hoped the power would be on by morning, and what's worse, the power company said it might take a few days. But only for some people. Who those people were was anybody's guess. I checked the power company website every two minutes, burning through my battery, panicked and wanting coffee something fierce. It was the worst storm in Omaha's history, with hurricane-force winds, causing the most power grid damage Nebraska had ever seen. Fortunately, there were no deaths, just destruction. When I looked outside, I saw several branches down in the neighborhood but nothing of particular concern. I was thankful we were safe and especially grateful the storm had cooled the temperatures outside.

But keeping two little girls entertained without electricity proved trying, and I wasn't particularly up for the challenge. They painted, played with their dolls, bounced a balloon around, put on a play with an empty cardboard box and a water bottle, until eventually begging us to watch TV.

"There's no power, baby," I told Poppy, who was feeling especially devastated.

"But my tablet died," she whined. "Can you plug it in?"

"My love, I told you. There's no power. Go play." But they had been, and you can only play with garbage for so long. She burst into tears and locked herself in my office. "Don't touch anything on my desk!" I called out.

The sun was out, but there's something about power outages that makes me feel limp and helpless. As if I must lie down until rescued. I've long known I'll be the first to go in an apocalypse, and I'm not happy about it either. In an emergency, it takes days to wade through my denial, and once I'm on the other side, it's too late. I lack urgency, and survival skills. And frankly, Rob is no better.

"Can you even start a fire without a match?" I asked him, while he drifted off to sleep next to me.

"What?"

"Yeah, I didn't think so," I said bitterly, crossing my arms.

The power still wasn't on forty-eight hours later, and we were paralyzed by indecision. We wanted to get a hotel room but worried that right as we checked in the power would come on. "I bet it's on by the afternoon," we'd say. "I bet it's on by this evening," we'd say. "I bet it's on by morning." And still no power.

By the third day, we'd had it. "Let's get a hotel room," I decided. "The girls can play at the pool, and I can finally get some writing done." But all the hotels were booked in Omaha and all the surrounding towns. Desperate, I checked for hotels in Lincoln, about an hour away, and found one hotel that had one room left. "Book it!" Rob shouted.

"Girls, let's pack," I announced like they were the next contestants on *The Price Is Right*. They'd been lying on the floor like picked carcasses and leaped up at the news.

"We're going to a hotel!" they screamed.

Both of my daughters consider going to a hotel to be the ultimate thrill ride. Forget amusement parks, Disney World, or cross-country adventures—all they need is a good Holiday Inn Express. Throw in the Cartoon Network, hotel snacks, and a complimentary breakfast, and wowza, the bliss is borderline pathetic.

The girls were buzzing as they packed. "Mommy!" Lucy called out from her room. "I'm bringing three pairs of undies, you know, just in case." Then she let out a short, crazed laugh.

"You go, girl!"

They packed their swimsuits, favorite clothes, and most beloved toys. We were all so fatigued from lying around helpless for days, the prospect of good food, air-conditioning, and charged devices felt like Christmas morning on crack cocaine. We piled into the car, and I took on the role as DJ, flipping through my favorite jams and cranking the music loud. We had nearly arrived at our hotel before I stopped to call my mom, letting her know what we were up to.

"Oh good, it's better for the girls," she said. "If you try to call in the next couple hours, I won't answer. Your father and I are leaving for Uncle Hank's celebration of life ceremony now."

My heart dropped. "Oh no, I totally forgot."

Uncle Hank died a couple of weeks after our visit, but due to COVID-19, they didn't have a funeral. Instead, they'd chosen to have a celebration ceremony in the summer, and while I knew the date, the lack of electricity made me forget the time, the day, the month, and that my period would start any minute. "What should I do? Come back? I haven't showered and put my makeup on by candlelight," I lamented. "I look like Alice Cooper. We don't have clean clothes . . ."

"No, no, we've just been through a terrible storm, and the venue doesn't even have power. It will probably just be his siblings attending. Check in and be safe," she assured me. But I felt terrible not going. Even though I'm not close with my cousin, for some reason I thought Chelsea might be hurt I wasn't there.

"Tell them a tree landed on our house, and we're buried under rubble," I said.

"I'm not lying for you; the truth is good enough."

"Okay, fine. Forget the part about the rubble."

"No."

My sister was in Colorado at her son's wedding, so I tried another tactic. "Okay, don't lie. Just say, 'They're in Colorado at Taylor's wedding.' Technically that's true, and they'll assume I'm lumped in."

"I'll do my fibbing best," she said.

"It's not a fib! You're just not being specific."

"Oh, right."

"But you have to say it just right or it won't work."

"Yes, got it."

"So, please practice in the car on your way there."

"Anna!"

I felt uneasy. My mom is a terrible liar, but there was nothing I could do. We moved into the city of Lincoln, and it was all lit up, like paradise. The girls were chirping in the backseat, laughing way too loud at jokes that weren't funny—the thing people do when they can't believe their good fortune. Just as we slid into the center of town, my phone beeped. It was my neighbor, celebrating, because the power was back on.

"Oh no," I said.

"What?" Rob asked.

"The power's back on."

"What?" Lucy asked. "We still going to the hotel, right, Mommy?"

"What do we do?" I asked Rob.

"They gave us special permission to cancel up until six, right? Do we really want to spend $250 for no reason? We're on a budget; your manuscript is due soon. We should cancel it and go home."

"What!" The girls shouted in unison.

"I'm so sorry, babies," I turned to tell them. "The power is back on; we need to go home. We'll make it up to you, I promise."

Crushed, they sat somberly in their car seats until we pulled up to our home. Lucy walked quietly into her room, locked the door, and wept. She buried her boo-hoos deep into her pillow, soaking it wet with tears. Similar, I imagined, to Aunt Beth's pillow, lying beside my uncle when he was there, but somehow gone.

I stood at Lucy's door as she cried. Her door was locked, but I could easily unlock it with my fingernail. After a moment's hesitation, I decided to give her privacy. Some things in life need the respect of a proper mourning, all the way through. As I walked back to my office to reply to some important emails, I thought it interesting how some tragedies move slowly, quietly, white-knuckled and dragging. Some blow in like a hurricane. And some are met with, perhaps, a little less drama. Something as simple as a joyful expectation unrealized.

After a few minutes, the sounds of her cry tapered. I heard the pitter-patter of a child's feet, the crank of the door handle, and the squeak of a door.

"Mama?" she said, standing in my office doorway.

"My baby." I spun my chair toward her and opened my arms. She came in close as I wrapped them around her. "I'm so sorry you are disappointed," I whispered in her ear. Behind me, I could feel her hand clawing, fumbling, and I heard the familiar thump of my phone hitting my desk. I pulled away, "What are you doing with my phone?"

"Can I play a game?" She grinned, cautious, dripping with charm.

I suppose, as it is with most tragedies, a moment will come when it's time to move on.

CHAPTER 3
Whoa Llama Llama

L lama Lady wore clear gloves that went all the way up to her midbicep. I'm sure that was intentional because she was elbow deep up the llama's hoo-ha.

It was hot and muggy in the barn, and I was sticky and miserable. I was just a little thing, no more than five years old or so, fresh and vulnerable. A few of us neighbor kids were usually invited to watch llama births. It was magic and terror rolled into one lazy afternoon.

We lived in the small, country town of Plattsmouth, Nebraska. A year prior, my family had moved there from Omaha—to have more land, horses, four-wheelers, and freedom, I guess. And we lived next to a woman who owned a llama farm. I remember her as quiet, thin, and plain, but maybe that's because her llamas were loud, fluffy, and ridiculous.

It was hard to get comfortable on the wooden bench in her barn. My upper lip was speckled with big drops of sweat that would drip to my lips, salty and cool. The smell of animals and poop clung in the air so thick you could let it slip through your fingers like a wisp of smoke.

As an adult, I've often wondered where one gets gloves up to your armpits without Amazon or Google. A vet catalog? Some farmer supply store? I envision the llama lady, thin and plain, approaching the clerk and asking for the special "up the wazoo" gloves. As the young clerk went to the back to check if they had some in stock, the llama lady would call out, "Get me the good ones, Randy! The off-brand gloves you gave me last time tore while I was in there, and no amount of soap got me clean!"

But I still question my memory. Do farmers normally birth their own animals? Don't they hire a vet? Maybe she *was* a vet? When I look through the lens of my memory, all I see is her right up in the poor llama's Mary-Ellen, and me, fidgety on a wooden bench, finding it a little hard to cope. All the other details are out of view.

My family lived on the outskirts of town, and every

so often my dad would drive us to Main Street. On the corner was a little store called Jack and Jill, and out front was a mechanical horse that would move back and forth, barely an inch either way. I'd beg my dad to let me ride. He'd help hoist me on and slip a quarter in. He'd get his quarter's worth, too, because it went on and on for at least five minutes. And I'd be up there, barely moving an inch either way, back and forth, back and forth with a stoic, self-assured expression on my face. My dad would wait patiently, holding his box of nails, masking tape, or this and that, and after the horse would come to a slow stop, I'd beg for another round. My dad cannot, for the life of him, say no, ever, to a child, so he dug into his pocket for another quarter and let me ride, squeaking back and forth, until sunset.

I attended a small three-room schoolhouse at the bottom of a large hill. It sounds quaint, like something right out of *Little House on the Prairie*, and appearance-wise it was. But it was just like other schools, just smaller with no resources or air-conditioning. Every weekday morning, I'd walk to school with a couple of my friends, and most of the time I'd have my collie, Lassie, with me (*real original name, Mom and Dad*). Sometimes she'd sit outside and wait for me to get out of school, and on hot days, when the teacher would open the door to help us get a breeze, Lassie would run in barking, running laps around my desk.

"Anna, tell Lassie to go home," my teacher, Mrs. Blue, snapped. But I was just five years old, what was I supposed to do about it?

"Lassie, go home!" I hissed. "Go on, go home!" But she'd

just sit there as I pulled on her collar, panting, barking, getting all frisky. I threw my hands up exasperated.

"Go get your brother then," she said, waving her hand. I was in the kindergarten/first-grade room, and Christian was in the fourth- and fifth-grade room across the hall. I'd knock and slowly creak the door open. Peeking my head in through the crack, the teacher stopped talking and looked at me. "Can Christian help me get Lassie home?" The teacher nodded, and Christian hopped up, following me back into my classroom. He immediately took command, grabbing Lassie by the collar and leading her out the door.

"Come on girl. Go home, you can't be in here," he said firm but sweet. Apparently, she respected him more than me and let him take her back outside. But she never went home. She curled up under the shade of the steps, waiting for the final bell.

I loved Mrs. Blue. She used to wear this peach-colored, Coca-Cola branded, long-sleeved rugby shirt on Fridays, and I thought it was the coolest. In my memory of her, I think of her in her early sixties, but when I recently asked my mom if that was accurate, she scoffed. "Oh, heavens no! I think she was in her late forties!" Since I'm almost forty now, that troubled me deeply. All I know is that Mrs. Blue treated us with love and kindness, and I was determined to be her favorite.

Although, looking back, I realize she used to do things that would probably put her in jail today. For example, during afternoon downtimes, while grading papers, she'd say, "Who wants to give me a shoulder massage?" and half the class would jump up and clamor for the opportunity like a bunch of weirdos. "Alright, alright, don't fight," she'd say, licking her finger, thumbing through papers. "You'll all get a turn. Just line up." So, I'd stand there, four kids deep, sighing with my hand on my hip. Perhaps it was just the times we were in, but massaging her shoulders didn't seem as grossly inappropriate as it does now. Truth was, my classmates and I lived for it, probably because we'd get rewarded with a Werther's Original after our turn was through. On one afternoon, after fighting for first in line, I massaged her shoulders with intention. My goal was simple: make sure she felt rejuvenated by the time I was done and remain her favorite until the end of time. But I was a couple squeezes in when I found myself in the midst of a dilemma. A giant sneeze tickled my nose, and there was no shooing it away. I didn't want to sneeze in my hand, then try and touch her again. That would be unseemly. And back then, sneezing into your elbow wasn't really a thing the Centers for Disease Control and Prevention was touting. What was I to do, blow it out on the back of her head? I shuddered at the thought. All I could think to do was hold my sneeze in, performing a sort of internal explosion, making this loud initial squeeze sound with no "choo" at the end.

"Baby girl, did you just hold your sneeze in?" she asked, looking over her shoulder.

"A little," I admitted.

"You're gonna blow your eyes out," she said casually, scrawling "Great job!" across a student's spelling paper.

I winced a bit at what felt like a criticism but continued on until it was time for Evie's turn. She handed me a Werther's, and I moseyed back to my desk. I felt satisfied enough at how the day was panning out until an hour later, when I found myself in the midst of another crisis. Maybe we all needed a nap, who knows, but the students in my class were losing their minds. Loud, laughing, slapping at each other, and ignoring the teacher's instruction. My anxiety grew up to my eardrums, watching the hellions disrespect our beloved Mrs. Blue. I sat there with my arms crossed, thoroughly disgusted by their behavior. Mrs. Blue's patience was running real thin as it was, then my friend Mike threw a spit wad across the room and she cracked. The entire class, except for me obviously, erupted in laughter. She slapped her book down with a loud thump. "That. Is. E-nough!" she shouted behind her desk. "I want complete silence for ten full minutes. Everyone put your heads down on your desk. And the next child to speak, raise their hand, or giggle will put their name up on the board *with a check*. Do we understand?" But I was glaring at Mike, judging him so severely for putting us in this horrific predicament that I missed the "Do we understand?" and raised my hand for clarification.

"Nope," she said, pointing at the board. "Go write your name up with a check, Anna. I clearly said no hand raising."

"But . . . ," my lip began to quiver.

"Do as I say, now go."

I went completely limp. Gobsmacked! And as she stood there with angry eyes, arm raised, and finger pointing at the board, my emotions rolled like crashing waves lapping onto the shores of my devastation. Never in my wildest nightmares could I have imagined joining the ranks of those naughty little street rats. Mike, Richard, and Jesse all had their names on the board with check marks to boot. After three checks, you got a letter sent home to your parents. I can't even talk about it without a cold chill. But checks were expected from these hellcats. I had never (not once!) had my name on the board, let alone with checks. My shame ran hot.

I got up slow and had to drag my increasingly limp body across the wood floor to the chalkboard. My arm was gummy like a noodle, and it took all my strength to grasp the chalk. *A-n-*, I looked back at Mrs. Blue in case she saw my misery and wanted to rescind her unjust discipline. To my despair, she wasn't even looking, filing a snag on her thumbnail. I turned back to the board, *n-a*—I looked back sorrowfully one last time, then—*Check.* I ran back to my chair, crossed my arms across my desk, and wept inside them bitterly.

Mrs. Blue sighed heavily, tossing her nail file into her desk drawer. "Anna, baby, come on. Come see me in the back room." The back room was a tiny closet where she stored school supplies, closed off by a curtain. I followed her behind the curtain, and she sat down, pulling me in for a hug. I wept dramatically onto her shoulder. "Now, I made it very clear that I didn't want a peep, not even a hand raise, or you'd have to put your name on the board. I have to follow through with the consequences I set for the class." I was sniffling over her shoulder when I saw Richard pull back the curtain, watching us. I looked him dead in the eyes and sneered. "It's alright, come on. Let's button up those tears," she said, patting my back.

"But, but, I didn't hear you say that! I was raising my

hand so you could repeat it," I wailed again, burying my head back into her shoulder.

"Well, you should have been listening," she said tenderly. "Now come on. Let's get back into class."

I nodded and took her hand before stopping, "Can I erase my name now?" I was hopeful my tears broke her down.

"Don't be silly," she said, giving my shoulder a squeeze. "Richard! Stop peeping in here! Look forward and put your head down!"

I followed her out of the storage closet and took a seat at my desk, where I laid my head down and sniffled for the remaining ten minutes. It's funny, the things we remember. The vast majority of our lives slip through the crevices of our memory, but certain things stick because for some reason, it mattered enough to stay. I'd been falsely accused, a victim of circumstance. Lassie running into my classroom, my inability to do anything about it. My name shakily written on the board. The hug in the back room. My inability to cry my way out of an unjust check. For the first time, I realized bad things can happen to good people. Even the class suck-up.

When the llama lady sounded the alarm that a baby was on its way, Mom called me down from my room and sent me right off by myself. As a mother of a five-year-old daughter myself, I can't imagine sending her off to get the mail at the end of the driveway by herself, let alone traversing the prairie to witness a live llama birth. But this was before the internet put us on a 24-7 terror loop, and most mothers were joyfully oblivious. I guess us moms just do the best we can in the era we live in.

Lassie walked with me over to her house. Whenever I was out walking around with Lassie, we were usually accompanied by another neighbor dog, a basset hound named Auggie. But he wasn't there with us that day, and I wondered where he could be. Maybe he was home inside, the day too warm.

As Lassie and I made our way, I tried to imagine what was in store for me. I naively assumed I would watch a llama writhe in pain on the straw-covered floor while a baby blew out her back end. But would there be snacks? Any fruit punch? Little Debbie snack cakes? Surely there'd be refreshments. *Right, Llama Lady?*

Lassie wasn't allowed in, so I left her at the gate. The first thing I noticed when I arrived were some neighbor kids, already sitting on a bench in the barn. The second thing I noticed was the lack of refreshments. I joined my friends, our sweaty arms rubbing up against each other, each of us a little nervous. I could really have used a snack, or at least a cold beverage. I don't know what kind of live birth event this lady was trying to put on, but I wasn't impressed!

The llama wasn't on the straw floor like I imagined, and while she adjusted her footing a bit more than normal, she stood tall and stoic. I was curious how this was all gonna go down, and even more curious as the llama lady put on the long, clear gloves. She wasted no time getting straight to business. She patted the llama's bottom and spoke gently to her before ever so gently sliding both arms into an area that shouldn't be able to handle one arm, let alone multiple arms. I was witnessing something impossible. Otherworldly. My eyes were round like saucers as sweat collected in the crease of my neck. My friends and I stared straight ahead; none of us made a sound. Frankly, this entire scenario felt out of my age range. Although adults were present, I had this feeling like no one was really looking out for me and my emotional well-being.

Then Llama Lady pulled. There was resistance, pivoting. The llama shuffled her feet and groaned. And then out came a slippery, slickery baby llama. She wobbled and crashed to the ground, then got up, straw stuck to her goopy body. She managed to wobble on all four hooves and stood. Her mother nuzzled her. Then the baby began to wobbly wobble and walk.

Just like that, something new that hadn't been there before appeared before my eyes. And it was walking! I sat, stunned, while still wishing I had a crisp Capri Sun to see me through.

I don't remember much else, but I do remember my walk home. I buzzed thinking about the new baby llama. So small, but so capable too. Walking and moving and nursing just moments after being born. Up ahead, I saw my brother playing catch with Lassie on our front lawn. I saw another neighbor dog running around them. The dog was some kind of mix—the lean active type that runs crazed for hours. But still no slow, clumsy basset hound.

"Where've you been?" Christian asked.

"I was at Llama Lady's watching a baby llama be born," I told him, tripping over some long grass.

"Really? Was it gross?" he asked playfully.

"I guess so," I told him, sparing him the details of Llama Lady and her gooped-up, arm-length gloves.

"Cool," he said, throwing the ball again.

"Have you seen Auggie?" I itched my right calf with my left foot.

"Oh, you haven't heard?" he asked, turning to look at me. I looked up and shook my head.

"Auggie died last week." He threw the ball. "Drowned in a pool."

A trickle of sweat spilled down my temple. I was barely old enough to grasp the new life I just watched enter the world and barely old enough to grasp that another had just left it.

My mind tried to envision him in the pool, his cute little body with his flappy long ears, somewhere at the bottom, but I wouldn't allow it and swatted the image away like a fly.

I walked up our drive and entered the house through the side, near the garage. Mom was in the kitchen, putting clean dishes into cupboards.

"Well, how was it?" she asked, on her tippy-toes, reaching high.

"It was neat," I said. I didn't have the language for what I'd experienced, so I kept it simple.

"That's it?" She stopped what she was doing and turned toward me.

"The baby was really cute and slickery and wobbly," I told her. I knew I had to throw her a few bones, or she'd never drop it. I wanted to ask her about Auggie—if she knew and kept it from me. Or maybe she had no idea. But for some reason, I decided against it. I didn't really want to talk about it anyway—I wanted to keep it for myself. To ponder it in my heart a little longer before an adult told me what it all meant.

I sat on my bed and tried not to think about Auggie. I pressed my fingers together and hummed the Itsy Bitsy Spider. The more I hummed, the less I thought about him floating in the pool. In my mind's eye, I see my white sheets, the handmade quilt on top. The way my feet looked swaying back and forth in front of me. Some moments slip through the crevices of our memory. Some things stick because they mattered enough to stay.

My friends and I grinning in a muggy barn. Clapping and laughing as a slippery newborn llama hobbled to her feet. Sweat trickling from our brows. All the while, Auggie was nowhere to be found. It was the first time I realized that bad things happen to good dogs. Even beloved basset hounds.

"Down came the rain and washed the spider out," I sang softly. My little hands whooshed down low, mimicking the little spider struggling, spilling to the ground. "Out came the sun and dried up all the rain," I placed my thumb to finger, finger to thumb, "and the itsy bitsy spider . . ." Up, up, up, my hands rose until they hung above my head, "crawled up the spout again." I took a big sigh and let my hands tumble from the sky.

The next morning, I'd tell Mrs. Blue all about my un-ordinary day. The fidgeting mama llama, the long gloves, the baby born before my very eyes. How I giggled as she fell into the hay. And of course, I mustn't forget, the disappoint-ing lack of refreshments.

I guess, for some reason, it mattered to me.

CHAPTER 4
Micky's Got a Gun

In the third grade, I'd stopped attending the three-room schoolhouse in Plattsmouth and started attending LaPlatte Elementary, a little school surrounded by homes that looked bleak and abandoned, even though people still managed to live in them. While we played four square and hopscotch during recess, off in the distance was a large nuclear power plant with plumes of steam billowing from the top of huge, unsightly towers. What's worse, we used to have "nuclear emergency" drills. The teacher handed us each a cloth diaper, and we'd huddle in the bathroom, covering our faces with the diapers. I don't remember feeling frightened; instead I recall getting a cheap thrill out of the experience. It was like a little field trip from the rigors of the classroom. "Now, put the cloth over your faces and stick your head between your legs, children," our teacher would tell us. I'd gladly follow instructions, giggling with my classmates. We're sitting on the sticky bathroom floor! So different! What fun!

"Why did you let me go to a crappy elementary school next to a nuclear power plant that could explode and kill me?" I asked my mom as a teenager. It was as if the injustice had just occurred to me, and I was deeply offended. "You're over here grinding your own grain, while I'm playing kickball next to toxic fumes?"

"The air was only toxic if it exploded," she said, putting Cascade into the dishwasher. "And it was the only elementary school in our district. What was I supposed to do?" She closed the dishwasher door. "You *loved it*, by the way."

She wasn't wrong. I really did love LaPlatte. It was small enough that our class grew up together, moving as a group into a new classroom, with a new teacher, each year. I'm still good friends with a good handful of my classmates today. It was also strangely socioeconomically diverse. The school was right in the middle of a rural, low-income area. But surrounding it were lakes and sprawling land, so it also attracted wealthy families.

One of my classmates was a quiet little girl named

Adrienne. She wore big round glasses, with a short haircut, pencil straight and perfectly cut bangs. Coincidentally, I too, had short hair with round glasses. Except my hair was curly, wilder, and probably washed less. Adrienne's dad was a doctor, and she was studious, polite, and very well behaved. But she was also a real good time. I'm still friends with Adrienne today, and one thing I've always loved about her is how easily she laughs at my jokes, no matter how raunchy or over the line. I know that's a very self-involved compliment to give someone, but if you think about it, what's better than being loved by someone who loves everything you have to say? In return, I soak up her goodness, and we enjoy each other's company. We should all be so lucky.

During the summer, I would stay at Adrienne's house for multiple days at a time. Adrienne's mom, Nancy, was usually on the NordicTrack skier, puffing away, watching daytime TV, when Adrienne would ask, "Can Anna stay one more day?" I'd be loitering behind her, pretending to be aloof either way. "If her parents are okay with it," Nancy would say, huffing along, rhythmically gliding back and forth with ease. "But aren't they missing her at home?" Honestly, I can't say they were. It wasn't neglect so much as me being the baby of the family and Mom moving into a new season of her life. If I wanted to spend another day at a doctor's house, what's it to her, really?

During one multiday stretch at Adrienne's during winter break, we decided to try out these new ski shoes Nancy had bought on a whim. They were like tiny sleds you strap to your feet. Nancy let me borrow her expensive snowsuit she'd wear skiing the slopes of Breckenridge, Colorado, but

49

she was a tiny, petite woman, and I was a robust, meaty child. Zipping me into it took a lot of elbow grease, and I grew increasingly self-conscious as Nancy grunted during the final stretch up to the top of the zipper. My coat at the time was one of my mom's hand-me-downs. At some point, there was a tear on the back, so my mom sewed on a large square patch from some leftover fabric to cover it. The square was off center, and its pattern was a conflicting moss green paisley. Mom was very stylish, so I'm quite sure she wouldn't have been caught dead in it with that ugly off-center patch. But I was just a kid, who cares? Saved her forty bucks on a new coat, at least.

Adrienne, in her sleek ski gear, and I, in her mom's tight ski pants and my ugly patch coat, huffed our way to the top of a big hill. I shuffled, stiff like a robot, one extended movement away from splitting Nancy's snowsuit clean at the crotch. I noticed I had to pee early on and felt the urge increase, but I was far too invested to turn back now. The labor of peeling out of head-to-toe winter gear, only to put it on all over again, was far beyond my tolerance threshold. I carried on.

As we approached the top of the hill, Adrienne volunteered to go first. She sat down in the snow and strapped her sled shoes onto her boots one at a time. But when she tried to stand up, she'd repetitively do the splits, as if she were on a giant block of ice. Helpless to assist out of fear I'd rip her mom's snowsuit if I bent over too far, I tried to offer tips that were no help at all. "Dig grooves into the snow and step inside those," I'd offer. Or, "Try to just stand up in one big swoop!" That was particularly bad advice because she went into the splits so hardcore, she had to rock back and forth on her pelvis to get a leg loose.

"Okay, I got this," she said, huffing and grunting, swinging her leg around for another go. After a few scrambles, she managed to stand straight up, but once her posture clicked, she took off down the hill like lightning. Adrienne screamed as if she were on a train that just hopped the rails, heading straight for a cliff. Her scream's pitch was one of pure terror, and it was truly the most hilarious vision I had ever seen. At one point, she tried to grab on to a tree limb to stop her momentum, but it only flipped her around and shot her down the hill backward.

"Just fall!" I yelled after her, but it was barely intelligible through my laughter. My belly laugh was so deep, there were moments I stopped breathing, scaring even myself. But for whatever reason, she was determined to remain standing, and I could hear her scream lessen as she squeezed smaller out of view. At the end of the hill, she exploded into a plume of snow dust. My laugh then lifted to a new dimension where I found myself on an alternate plane of existence.

That's when it happened.

At first, it was just a small amount of pee. The slightest little dribble, barely worth mentioning. But that dribble signaled to the rest of my body that it was game on. I clinched and tightened best I could, terrified by what was happening. But then I caught a glimpse of Adrienne trying to get up at the bottom of the hill, now doing front to back splits like she was James Brown in concert. No amount of clenching could hold back the floodgates that burst so wide open, all

I could do was lie back and accept it. *It's happening*, I cried. *I'm peeing now*. Once it started, there was no stopping it. I sat on the snow, fell to my back, and released my entire bladder into Nancy's snowsuit. At first it felt nice and warm, but it took mere moments to grow wet and cold. Then more pee came, running and running, soaking and drenching. It was so unimaginable to pee my friend's mother's pants, I actually felt nothing at all. Numb and urine soaked.

Adrienne finally got wise and took off the shoe sleds. She marched back up the hill, while I still lay motionless, just peeing. Slowly, gently. "Did you see that?" she asked, nearly out of breath.

"Oh, I saw it," I said, hopeless. A corpse.

"There's no way you're putting these on," she said, throwing them down into the snow. "I could have hit a tree and died!" She plopped down next to me, furious her mom had endangered us with those death boots. It took a few beats for her to notice I wasn't quite myself. "You okay?"

"I just peed," I told her.

"What's that?"

"I just peed. Like, for real peed. Right into your mom's snow pants."

"I'm sure it's fine—"

"Adrienne, trust me," I interrupted. "It's bad." This was a worst-case scenario; how could I possibly go on? My mind rummaged for ways out of my predicament, but I was a child! What could I do? There were no cell phones to secretly beg my sister to pick me up and whisk me away, to mercifully never see Adrienne or her family again. The only possible path was to face the facts. The raw truth was this: I borrowed my friend's mom's expensive name-brand ski pants and peed in them, helplessly, like a toddler. The only thing left to do was walk like a toy soldier back to the house and meet my fate. Unless, of course, I could stall and come up with a plan.

"Please, don't tell your mom," I begged. "Maybe we can pat these dry. Lather them in soap. There has to be something we can do!"

"She doesn't have to know," Adrienne assured me. Sweet, kind Adrienne, willing to help me cover up my humiliating crime. We slowly made our way back to her house. My gait was now more like a toy solider waddling in peed fatigues. We took our boots off in the garage, where I noticed even my socks were soaked. We opened the door into the house slowly. There was no mother to the north, or south. We ran through the kitchen, then sprinted up the stairs into Adrienne's bedroom. We shut the door, and with her help, I was able to peel out of the snow pants. To my relief, I had packed an extra pair of underwear and green jogging pants. I changed into them quickly, then observed the pee pants on the ground as my mind raced to find a solution. *Maybe they don't really smell like pee*, I considered. I picked them up, took a huge whiff, then blew my head back in disgust. "These stink so bad," I told her. "What are we gonna do?"

Neither of us knew how to use a washing machine, so it was time to explore Adrienne's higher-than-average IQ. "I know," she offered. "Let's spray them with air freshener and hang them up in the guest bedroom." It wasn't foolproof, but it had merit, so we went on a hunt for the air freshener. We snuck around on our tiptoes, dashing behind corners as her mom would walk by, searching through every cupboard in the house. Unable to find it, we went to plan B: perfume.

"You got any perfume?" I whispered as we hid behind the kitchen island while her mom got herself a glass of water. "Jōvan White Musk? Anything?"

"I have Ex'cla-ma'tion," she whispered. "Will that work?" Not my favorite fragrance, but what choice did we have? It had to work. Adrienne and I slid back upstairs and doused the pants in perfume until the fumes gave us a mild head-ache. Her bedroom reeked, unsurprisingly, as if someone at Walgreens who had just peed their pants picked up the Ex'cla-ma'tion perfume tester and doused themselves from head to toe. With bated breath, we looked both ways out of her room before scurrying into the guest bedroom. We hung my greatest shame in the closet, closed the door, and breathed a huge sigh of relief. We did it. Nancy would never know I peed her expensive ski pants. We were so confident, in fact, we moved on swiftly from the drama, heading back to the kitchen to fix ourselves a little snack.

At the start of sixth grade, we noticed a new girl sitting in our midst. She was country mixed with a little sass, wearing bedazzled cowboy boots with Levi's. Her name was Micky, and it didn't take long to figure out she wasn't well behaved. Unlike me, who often walked a tightrope between cementing my place as teacher's pet and navigating the politics of popularity, she clearly didn't care about any of it, dropping swear words and strutting around. Lawless.

She scared me a little. Even a young child can sense the threat of someone with nothing to lose. The boys picked up on this early and tried to live out their rebellion vicariously through her. They didn't bully Micky, per se, but mostly used her, egging her on to do wild things they were too scared to do. I can't say I was completely innocent. In my heart, I knew it was wrong, but there was a sort of white-knuckled, edge-of-your-seat excitement watching someone do things you couldn't fathom doing yourself. It was permission to live wild, crazed, and free while incurring none of the consequences. I'd get whipped up, giggling and laughing, engrossed by how it all might end.

Over time, it was obvious Micky would do anything the boys dared her to do. She was so fearless, it felt exciting and threatening at the same time. One day they dared her to pee on the bus. Easy. She'd squat down off her seat, and I'd gag and screech as pee rolled back and forth down the aisles. The boys laughed. Our bus driver, an old gentleman, looked ahead, making his way through country roads.

Another morning, while our teacher was busy flipping through papers before the first bell rang, the boys told Micky to put her boots underneath the closet door and then hide behind a bookshelf. When our teacher began class, my friend Brett raised his hand. "Um, Mrs. Aboe? Micky's in the closet, and she won't come out."

Mrs. Aboe sighed and put her hands on her hips. She was clearly too tired and too underpaid. "Micky, come on out of there," she said, her voice raised. When her command was followed by silence, she upped the ante. "Micky, come on out, *right now*. I mean it. You'll go straight to the principal's office. Let's go!" When that command was met by mostly silence and a few giggles from the classroom, she huffed over to the closet and ripped open the sliding door. She was met with nothing but a pair of cowboy boots. The classroom erupted with laughter, and I felt a ping of sympathy for Mrs. Aboe. I was just a little girl, but even I knew getting pranked by a bunch of kids had to be humiliating. "Where is she?" she asked us, her cheeks flush. "On the count of three!" None of us knew what would happen at the end of three, but a few of us weren't about to find out.

"Behind the bookshelf!" a cluster of us shouted. Micky rose with a smirk and made her way back to her desk.

"Oh no you don't!" Mrs. Aboe yelled. "To the principal!"

I'm afraid that was just the tip of the iceberg. Before Christmas break, Mrs. Aboe had taken some class pictures and was struggling to replace the film. There was a tiny storage closet in our classroom, so she slipped inside so she could fix the problem without exposing the film. Right as the door clicked, a cluster of boys looked at Micky and hissed "Lock her in!" Without skipping a beat, Micky popped up and slid a chair under the door handle. A rash instantly hit my chest and crawled up my neck. Within seconds, Mrs. Aboe tried the door handle and realized she'd been blockaded in.

"Open this door!" she shouted. My palms began to sweat, and the room spun. This was truly naughty business, and I felt clammy and nauseated. The door rattled aggressively, and she pounded the door. "Open this door, *now*!" Half the class erupted in laughter as the door rattled against the chair, and Micky giggled, pressing her back end up against the chair to ensure it didn't move. Mrs. Aboe grew more desperate, pounding on the door, screaming for us to open it. I wouldn't be surprised if she thought she might die in there. It didn't take long for our giggles to slowly fade, replaced by a sense of impending doom. *What's the endgame here?* we all seemed to wonder. At some point, this would have to end. And when it did, what would become of us?

I can't really tell you what happened next, because the unbelievable naughtiness of it all caused me to black out after the first thirty seconds, but I've been told by classmates that after Mrs. Aboe's audible meltdown, a few brave students spoke up and demanded Micky remove the chair. Once Micky noticed she was outnumbered, she did as she was told, and Mrs. Aboe spilled from the closet. She brushed her dress down, her face red, sweat collecting at her brow.

"Oh, y'all are in some big trouble." She was so enraged, we could barely make out the words. Her jaw and her fists were clenched tight as she walked slowly to her desk. Her gait, methodical. Measured. Looking back, it reminds me of a scary movie when a psychopath has accepted their impulse to murder. They become calm, steady. An insane look in their eyes. Resolve.

Luckily, after sitting at her desk with her back turned to the class, she was able to collect herself and avoid beating us all senseless. After what must have been fifteen minutes, she turned her chair toward us. "Micky, get up. I'm taking you to the principal myself." Micky popped up, grinning at us as she left the room.

I was on another multiday visit at Adrienne's house when the phone rang. It was Micky's mom, hoping Adrienne could come over and play. But when she heard I was over, she invited me too. Neither Adrienne nor I really wanted to go. We'd heard rumors about Micky's mom—mostly that she was a mean, nasty, abusive woman. In our minds, we conjured up visions of a horrid, wicked witch—the reason why Micky was the way she was. But Nancy wasn't privy to the rumors and encouraged us to visit for a little while. When we protested, she told us it was the right thing to do, and we needn't stay very long.

Micky lived within walking distance from Adrienne's house, so we made our way over, through trails and gravel roads, nervous and unsure about what "playing at Micky's" would actually be like. I envisioned they lived in some kind of derelict home out in the middle of nowhere, so I was surprised when her large, nice country home revealed itself through a patch of trees. Four-wheelers were parked out front. Horses nibbled on grass in the back. As we got closer, we could hear the mom screaming and dropping f-bombs at Micky's younger brother, Andy, and both Adrienne and I tensed up. The rumors were true, she really was scary. And we were the baby lambs being led to slaughter!

Micky opened the door before we were able to knock. As the door creaked open, we stepped in like Hansel and Gretel, looking for the witch. Micky's mom was visible from the kitchen, but she didn't acknowledge us. I thought it was weird. Hadn't she been the one to call on Micky's behalf? *Was this a trap?*

"Come up to my room," Micky said. We followed her

up the stairs and could still hear her mother cussing out Andy in the kitchen. I suppose in her mom's defense, Andy was a real hellcat. He was the kind of kid who'd try to kill the neighbor's cat and tell you to go screw yourself if you confronted him about it. On the other hand, their parenting probably had something to do with that, so round and round we go.

I wasn't frightened by the yelling and cursing, but I was uneasy. It was one of my first indications that the world can be unsafe. That parents aren't always a refuge, or a child's everything—the lap you crawl into, while loving hands hold you. Your parents can actually be your nightmare, the very thing you try to run from but can't. Where could Micky go?

Her bedroom wasn't anything to write home about. Neither girly nor a pit. Just a room filled with hand-me-down blankets, a beat-up chest of drawers. A few of her favorite things were hung on the wall, with no particular rhyme or reason to their display. I could hear one of the four-wheelers rumble on, and through the window I saw Micky's mom pull out of the driveway. I assumed it was to tend to some animals, or maybe pay a visit to a neighbor. A sense of relief washed over me with her out of the home. Micky peeked outside her window and watched until her mother was out of view. "Follow me, I want to show you something," she told us. Adrienne and I shared glances. Coming from Micky, we knew we were being led to something unsavory. She wasn't taking us to her playroom to show her handmade dollhouse—this was going to steal our innocence. That much was clear.

My chest muscles clenched when I saw she was taking

us in her parents' bedroom. Their room, like Micky's, was also plain and uninteresting. A brown, old comforter and worn, old sheets. A chest of drawers, likely a hand-me-down from an aunt looking to get rid of it, with a cheap picture of a sailboat on the wall. As she led us toward the closet, I looked carefully out of the windows for any sign of her mom. "Micky, we shouldn't be here," Adrienne muttered. She was clearly terrified. So was I, but I had a bit more tolerance for this kind of thing. I had more edge and less naivete. Although both Adrienne and I grew up in safe, loving homes, she was the oldest child, with an inherent temperament to follow the rules and do the right thing. All of this naughtiness, crudeness, and meanness were truly brand new. As the youngest in my family, I had witnessed my brother and sister grow into teenagers; I hadn't seen it all, but I'd seen a few things.

We followed Micky into a small walk-in closet where, hidden underneath a pile of clothes, there was a large wooden box. Micky scaled the wall, using the box to give her height and leverage. She stretched long, patting her hand around the top shelf before coming down with a key. Then, from her pocket, she put on a pair of black gloves. Once the gloves were put on, alarm bells banged around in my head. *Does she not want her prints on this box?* I wondered. Who would even dust for prints? I resigned myself. *I'm about to see a dead body.*

She put the tiny key into the lock and slowly lifted the wooden lid. I was lightheaded until I realized I was holding my breath. The first thing I noticed was Madonna's book, *Truth or Dare. Oh*, I thought to myself. *That's it?* The book was certainly raunchy and inappropriate for us to peruse but wasn't exactly pornographic. We flipped through some of the pages, alarmed and fascinated, but overall our innocence remained somewhat intact. It wasn't until she removed the book and set it aside that I realized we were truly in a closet of horrors. First, she revealed nude pictures of her parents and various other strangers engaged in acts we didn't quite understand. Mercifully, the photos were worn-out Polaroids, so it was like looking through a foggy window. What my eight-year-old mind surmised was that her parents were in some kind of naked group for unattractive country folk. My synapses were firing. *Adults do dirty things outside of marriage! And it's even scarier when everyone is super gross!*

Adrienne grew quiet and withdrawn, looking around the closet and refusing to focus on anything in particular. Micky then set the photos aside and pulled out a bag of a white powdery substance she identified as cocaine. "You guys wanna try it?"

"No!" Adrienne yelled. "Put it back, Micky! Put it away right now!" All I could do was stand there stunned. Even though I wasn't fully educated on the breadth of drugs, I did know drugs were real bad. I even think I had a D.A.R.E. shirt tucked way somewhere in my closet. Drugs equaled jail, death, crime, and a mouth without teeth—and there they were, in my midst!

Adrienne and I backed away from the bag of crack and pictures of ugly naked people, spilling out of the closet. While Micky's hands were safely confined in gloves, our fingerprints were now on everything. Everything! What if the FBI raided this place? Adrienne and I weren't suited for juvie; we'd never survive it, that much was obvious. "Okay, Micky, that's enough. We don't need to see any more," I protested. "Let's go now, okay?"

Micky grinned. The same kind of grin she shot at the class when Mrs. Aboe would send her off to the principal. A grin that said, "I can do anything I want, because I'm not afraid of the consequences. And I bet it scares you." And it did. Deep down she scared all of us.

Especially when Micky brought out a huge handgun, gripped tightly inside her gloved hand. Adrienne screamed, the kind so high pitched it rattles your soul. We both hit the floor, our hands over our heads.

"Put it down, Micky! Put it down!" Adrienne wailed. I could tell through the waver of her voice that she was about to cry. But she kept screaming.

"Calm down," Micky said matter-of-factly. She waved the gun around recklessly above our heads. "I won't shoot you." As if that was supposed to be comforting? It was then we heard the familiar sound of a four-wheeler pulling into the driveway. Micky ran to the window, saw her mom, and hissed, "We gotta get out of here, go, go, go!" Adrienne screamed again, wild and hysterical, as we both practically dive-rolled down the stairs and out the front door.

"You girls leavin' already?" Micky's mom asked us as we fled past her in the driveway.

"Yeah, sorry. Bye!" Adrienne shouted behind her. We ran, all the way home. Through the forest, up the trail, on the gravel road, and up the large hill her home sat upon. Once we got close and felt safe, we slowed to a walk, our chests heaving, sweat on our upper lips. I had my hand on my hips—I wasn't built for that kind of sustained exercise. We walked in silence; neither of us dared say a word. The closet was beyond anything either of us had ever known in real life—everything we'd been taught to flee from. Drugs. Illicit sex. Violence. It was far too much for two little girls who weren't ready to know about such things.

We walked into the house through the garage, where we met Nancy in the kitchen.

"Back so soon?" she asked us, wiping down the countertop.

"Yeah," was all Adrienne offered.

We made our way up into Adrienne's bedroom. Each step slow, both of us mourning the slice of innocence that just slipped through Micky's gloved hand.

"Oh, girls?" Nancy called up to us from the bottom of the stairs. We turned together and looked at her. "I found my snow pants." She held them up, still clinging off the hanger. Her eyes narrowed; her lips curled. "I'd been wondering where they were."

Adrienne and I met eyes, then looked back at Nancy. She knew. We knew. But she was gracious and let us continue up the stairs without explanation. We crawled into Adrienne's four-post bed, exhausted and a little weepy. "I want to go home now," I said to her, sprawled out on the bed, looking up at the canopy above. "I think my family misses me now."

"It's okay," Adrienne said. I got up to call my mom then crawled back up on the bed. We lay side by side quietly, our minds running, until we heard a comforting sound.

A car pulling into the driveway.

CHAPTER 5

First Day

L acy and I were dead asleep when the phone rang. Her
   dad, Merle, had long gone to work, so she ignored it,
both of us changing positions, sighing heavily as a response
to the obnoxious, incessant noise. Finally, the racket stopped,
but within seconds the phone's ring picked up again. In most
cases, this is a warning the call pertains to something serious.
Unless, of course, it's me calling my mom to wax poetic about

how I might be into capris again, and she has the audacity to be doing something, anything, other than waiting by the phone in case I call. One time I called thirteen times until she finally answered and said, "My God, is someone dead?" To which I replied, "What? No. But I think running is making my calves big because some of my pants are getting tight. Should I quit running or just accept my man calves?"

Lacy got out of bed once the rings picked up again, making her way to the phone. "Hello? Oh, hi," she said, groggily, rubbing her eyes. "Oh, it is? Uh-oh . . . uh-huh, okay. Yes, she brought clothes, I think. Okay . . . uh-huh. Bye."

"Who was that?" I asked, peeking my head above the covers.

"Your mom. It's the first day of school, and we're late!"

So typical. Yes, I was the baby of the family by at least five years, but had we given up? We're all moving on with our lives and forgot that one of us still needs an adult to keep an eye on the calendar? My sister, now working the Estée Lauder counter, my brother now driving, my mom now working, and my dad never involved with school stuff to begin with—but hello! *There's still a child in the family who needs someone to know when school starts.*

Unfortunately, the only pair of clothes I brought in my overnight bag left a lot to be desired for first-day-of-sixth-grade fashion, but beggars can't be choosers. I threw on bright green jogging pants and a raggedy pink T-shirt with a teddy bear on it. I brushed my hair, forwent my teeth, and Lacy and I ran outside the minute we heard my mom pull into the driveway.

"What about our backpacks?" I asked my mom as she peeled out backward.

"It's the first day; you don't need your backpacks." Then she gunned it, our heads blowing back against the back seat of her Buick. I'm not sure what Merle's excuse was, other than he was a gruff, but kind, single father who probably relied on cues from our family to know when school started. Big mistake. Mom had begun working for the first time in a long time, so she was distracted on her new venture, and in general was never strict or micromanaged our schooling anyway. If I didn't want to go, she wouldn't resist, and I'd spend the day watching daytime TV, baking and eating my own tater tots if she wasn't home, and dipping each one into ketchup with smug satisfaction. Looking back, I'm certain I far surpassed what was allowed in school absences, but maybe schools back then cared less? "Two hundred dollars!" I'd yell at the woman standing next to Bob Barker. True, I had no idea how much a refrigerator cost, but it couldn't be *that much*. At any rate, my grades were fine overall, so I guess Mom thought, *Whatever*.

After our Indy 500–style ride to school, Mom screeched into the parking lot. I wasn't pleased with my outfit; I hadn't brushed my teeth and barely got a comb in my hair. My generation takes professional photos of our little one on the first day of school, dressed up to the nines, with a cute little chalkboard to let the entire world know what grade our angels are entering. Aren't we all so proud?

After kindergarten, I don't recall ever having a first-day-of-school photo. But even though that was the '80s and, in general, our moms didn't give a crap, I could tell forgetting my first day wasn't a good look. I sensed it by how Mom seemed flustered. "Have fun!" she called out to us through the window. Then she almost got out of the car, as if she wasn't sure if she should explain our tardiness or just avoid the whole thing altogether. Lacy and I turned and waved and soon discovered she was just going to let this one go. She drove off, making her way down the winding road.

We walked in the building, nodded to the secretary, and turned into the sixth-grade class.

"Well, here they are!" Mrs. Aboe said. "Come on in, girls."

"How'd you guys forget the first day of school?" our classmate Brett asked. I shot him eye darts and took a seat.

"We were just going around talking about our summers," Mrs. Aboe said. "We'll come back to you girls when we finish the circle."

Despite my parents' lack of leadership in the education arena, I still wanted to excel for excelling's sake, and I really didn't appreciate my mom setting me up for embarrassment. I had a classmate named Bubba; his birth name, not his nickname—and the woman who named him Bubba somehow managed to know when school started! I crossed my arms in displeasure, but as I watched my classmates share their summers, not even one seemed to be thinking about how late we were for our first day of school.

I guess, maybe, it wasn't a big deal.

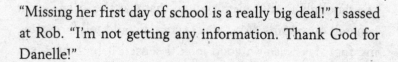

"Missing her first day of school is a really big deal!" I sassed at Rob. "I'm not getting any information. Thank God for Danelle!"

I'm not sure what I thought would happen. I guess I assumed that someone from somewhere would contact me about enrolling Lucy into school and then guide me through a quick and easy step-by-step process. Lucy was still in pre-K, and my mind wasn't even flirting with kindergarten thoughts when Danelle asked, "Did you enroll Lucy into school yet?"

"Hubba what?" I answered with a huge hunk of a sub sandwich in the back of my throat. "It's not even February, what are you talking about?"

"I just remember the enrollment with Sloane started around this time, so you should look into it."

Look into it? *How*? I often amaze myself by all the things I've accomplished in my life, and yet I get hung up on things like "enrolling my child into elementary school." Is there a main website hub of some sort where I can access this information? Do I just pick a school? How do I know which one is in my district? Can I choose another one? Where do I go? What do I google? SOMEONE JUST DO THIS FOR ME, I HATE IT.

Thankfully, finding the district's website and subsequent enrollment links proved to be less challenging than I feared. Luckily for us, we have an elementary school in our neighborhood, and the walk is on a quaint, tree-lined street. Except for the one dilapidated house where the owner mows bimonthly and leaves empty fast-food bags in his driveway, our walk is scenic, peaceful, and perfect. I found our school from a drop-down menu, followed all the steps, and after roughly five hours of mind-numbing bureaucratic paperwork, Lucy was officially enrolled at her elementary school. Or at least, that's what the email said after I hit "submit."

I found myself with some time on my hands, so I poked around the school's website. I discovered it was one out of a select few schools that touted a rigorous, unconventional curriculum. I must say, I bristled at the word "rigorous." If a kindergartener goes to a "rigorous" school, what it actually means is that things are about to get real "rigorous" for me, who's going to be expected to keep up the rigor at home. All I wanna do after dinner is take my bra off, not recite phonograms! Besides, are they not mere babes? When I was in kindergarten, I painted pictures and tried not to pee my pants. Why is the school threatening me like this?

On a positive note, the online feedback I read for the school's particular curriculum had raving reviews, and although I wasn't stoked about more homework for her that, let's be real, is also homework for me, I was impressed she'd be able to read Tolstoy's *Anna Karenina* by the end of the school year. Still, I had my doubts.

I walked into the family room where Rob was relaxing on the couch and read him the curriculum's description. "Don't you think this is a bit much?" I asked him. "In kindergarten, I went home at noon after a full morning of picking my nose and gluing papers together. And look at me now—a published author!"

"I mean, the school's just a few blocks away," Rob said, pragmatically. "Do we really want to drive her to another school so she can learn less?"

"Okay, fine," I said, standing up in a huff. "But if at any point in the school year I start crying while Lucy does her homework because it's too much for me, she's transferring."

"You mean Lucy?"

"What?"

"You mean, if Lucy starts crying?"

"What?"

"Never mind," he said, going back to an article about Texas football. "You know, I can help. You realize that, right?" I turned around and walked away because we both knew that was nonsense. When dinner's been eaten and the day winds down, this would, one way or another, fall on me. Not because Rob isn't capable or is unwilling to take on any of the family responsibilities. In fact, he's truly a fifty-fifty partner when it comes to parenting together. But it's not him, it's me. I *want* the home and our schedules to be my domain. I like the house to run a certain way because it relieves my stress instead of adding to it. Rob, who isn't burdened by the need for a tidy home or schedule, will, understandably, want to help with homework when *he feels like it*. But I would like him to help with homework when *I want the homework done*. I don't want the hassle of controlling him as if he isn't a grown man with his own agency, so it's better to just be controlling from the get-go and do it myself.

And this meant, in due time, I'd need to brush up on my phonograms. Control does have its consequences.

"Lucy Thomas," I told the PE teacher, muffled through my mask. To be fair, I wasn't completely sure he was the PE teacher; he just had PE teacher vibes. Physically fit, wind pants dressed up with a nice polo, Oakley sunglasses, lots of energy, that sort of thing. It was scorching hot outside, and I was miffed at myself for lathering on my pricey lip gloss, just to put a mask on top of it. We were under a tent for an awkward Kindergarten Welcome COVID Protocol Extravaganza, where we received a welcome packet from a safe distance. Truth be told, I was a little annoyed. I didn't get any type of email or notification about the event; I had just happened to stumble upon the dates when checking the website.

The PE teacher flipped through his paper looking for Lucy's name, back and forth, back and forth, and it put me on edge. This wasn't my first rodeo—I know the signs. We weren't on the list. From as far back as I can remember, my name, and usually *only* my name, is left off lists. It's so consistent that I've had to examine my thought and behavior patterns to see if I've somehow manifested this deep inconvenience in my life without knowing it. "Hmm, how do you spell your last name?" is usually some last-ditch effort in hopes they mistook "Thomas" for "McGillicuddy" before they speak to someone in authority, hushed and out of earshot. The most egregious incident is when I drove across the country for a new job at a university, and when I attempted to register on campus, there was no evidence I was hired, or even existed at all. At orientation, all my new coworkers had their names dangling on lanyards, carrying huge training binders and bags filled with campus swag. All I had was my purse and a deep-seated fear someone made a huge mistake.

Maybe it shouldn't be, but discovering you're absent from a list feels a bit degrading. The pharmacist at Walgreens who can't find "a prescription under that name." My friend who put me on the list to go backstage yet the bouncer points to the back of the line, and my walk of shame, of course, as I do so.

As I stood in front of Lucy's school under the tent, it was evident I was in for another degrading experience. Lucy began to fidget under the pressure, adjusting her mask.

"Hmm, how do you spell your last name?" the PE teacher asked.

"Thomas, T-H-O-M-A-S," I replied, holding Lucy's hand tight.

"Hold on a sec." He then slipped away toward a woman I recognized as the principal from the school's website. After they had their back and forth, hushed and out of earshot, she came over to the table with a smile behind her mask. "Hello, Lucy!" She then turned to the PE teacher. "She's on the list," she said to him in a robust tone, then quietly added, "Just write her name in." She looked at me, "Could you add your email address next to your name?"

I eyed her suspiciously, but at least she didn't say, "I'm sorry, we don't have any record of your child, and we're all out of room. Have you tried registering her at another school?" or some other such nonsense I most definitely didn't have time for. So, I accepted her word, and we hightailed it out of there before someone realized there'd been a mistake.

Lucy and I walked home, hand in hand, talking about what would be in store for her in kindergarten. I was relieved Lucy would receive in-person learning for her first year but was devastated she'd have to experience it all behind a mask. Although I knew masks were a necessary precaution in public, I hated them. The way they inhibited my breathing gave me anxiety—this sense I needed to hurry my shopping so I could run out of the building and peel it off. But when I asked Lucy how she felt, she seemed to be okay. If her mask was cute and her friends wore one, it didn't seem to be an issue. After a time, I realized my baby wearing a mask in school seemed to bother me more than it bothered her, at least for now. I had to let my worry ease and flow like a gentle stream away from me. This was a difficult time, made more difficult by my inner resistance it was even happening at all.

My parents recall school drills where they hid under desks while under threat of a nuclear bomb. I hid in the bathroom with a cloth diaper covering my face under threat of a nuclear power plant near my school. And my Lucy had to wear a mask under threat of a virus. Each generation tends to think the world has gone to hell in a handbasket, that our generation truly has it the worst. But that's mostly because we have terrible memories about what was in previous handbaskets. It's because life does move on, and so do we. Most things do get better. I let myself believe it as my worry flowed away from me. Trickling, babbling through time.

Overall, the communication from the school left me wanting. As Lucy's first day of school approached, I didn't hear a single word from anyone. My friend, Danelle, whose daughter was in the same district, would call and say things like, "Skip the Target near you; the school supply aisle's been raided." To which I'd reply, "Thanks for the tip. But, um, ahem, and I totally know the answer to this, but do you know what supplies we're supposed to get? Hold on, let me get a pen."

Intellectually, I knew I needed to pick up school supplies, but I assumed the school would prompt me with an announcement of some sort. "You didn't get an email?" she asked. And when I said no, she said, "There should be a link on the school's website. If not, I'll send you ours." Okay, thanks, but none of that soothed my concerns that I was really fending for myself. The resources were there if I went looking for them, but this was my first baby in kindergarten! I know I should theoretically be taking responsibility for myself and next of kin, but a little hand-holding the first year really isn't too much to ask. Is it?

On her first day, I patiently waited in line behind cars that were quite literally doing whatever they felt like doing, teacher in the crosswalk be damned, and found a place to park. Lucy and I walked up to the front doors. The woman standing beside them asked, "Who's her teacher?"

"Mrs. Wicks?" The only reason I knew who her teacher was, is because, mercifully, Mrs. Wicks had emailed all the parents a couple days before school started. The email still seemed to be lacking important, helpful information though. She wrote as if she assumed I already knew all I needed to know, and she was just recapping the most important parts. Wrong!

"Oh, you'll be using the side door for Mrs. Wicks's class," she said, pointing to the edge of the building. "You'll see it once you turn the corner." We made our way around, and Lucy picked up vibes I had no idea what I was doing.

"Do you know where it is, Mama?" she asked with big, fear-filled eyes.

"Of course I do," I replied. Of course, I was lying, but I

assumed we'd figure it out eventually. We saw a staff member up ahead near a door, and I deduced she was our ticket in. "Kindergarten? Mrs. Wicks?" I asked as we approached.

"First day!" the woman shouted. "How exciting! Come on in, I'll show you to your class." I squatted, pulled down our masks, and smooched my Lucy.

"You have the most wonderful day," I said to my first baby. Lucy grinned, we said our "I love yous," and off she went with the teacher, disappearing down the hallway.

The first week went smoothly. I made her lunches, mostly because I had no idea how you buy hot lunches, and although she continually rebuffed my killer sandwiches, she seemed to eat everything else. All I had to do was drop her off at school and pick her up, and that much I could do.

On her second week, I pulled into the pickup lane and noticed students were streaming out of the building wearing various silly hats. I wondered if it had to do with a particular grade until I saw Lucy exiting behind Mrs. Wicks with a sense of urgency. When she got in the car in the pickup lane, I shouted, "How was your day?" with an over-the-top enthusiasm she didn't have time for.

"Good. But Mommy, I didn't have a fun hat today like I was supposed to," she said, exasperated. "And we're supposed to wear blue tomorrow for spirit."

"You're supposed to wear blue for spirit?"

"Yes."

"*Okay*. Well, you don't have a blue shirt, do you?"

"No!" I could feel her desperation. "I need a blue shirt, Mommy! Why don't you know this?"

Why don't I know this, indeed. "So, tomorrow you're supposed to wear a blue shirt? That's it?"

"No. Then another day we have fun socks, and another day we wear pajamas, and then . . . and then . . . I forget the other days!" She was on the brink of collapse. Here, a small child; a mother, useless! Where could she turn? Who could she trust with her emotional and academic well-being?

I flushed hot. I had a busy evening ahead of me, and now I needed to make an inconvenient Target run for a blue shirt and fun socks. But also, am I supposed to take a five-year-old's word for it? I'm still helping to wipe her butt on the rare occasion things get out of hand—I need more to go on than her panicked utterings. Once we got home, I emailed Mrs. Wicks, who, thankfully, responded quickly and confirmed that it was, indeed, Spirit Week.

"I didn't receive any information about this—am I missing newsletters or something?" I typed quickly then fired off my phone.

"Yes, there is a newsletter that goes out weekly that had this information. Contact the front office if you aren't receiving them," she replied. "They can help make sure you're getting the information you need."

Aha! So, I was right to be suspicious when my name was added haphazardly to a piece of paper at the Kindergarten COVID Protocol Extravaganza. I contacted the front office, and the woman who answered the phone assured me I was now added to the school's email list; as confirmation, I received the newsletter with information on Spirit Week. I breathed a sigh of relief before breathing a sigh of annoyance, as I headed to Target to purchase thirty-five dollars' worth of last-minute blue shirts and crazy socks. Turns out, Target really doesn't have crazy socks, so Lucy just got nice knee socks instead. *And I better not get no lip!*

With that crisis averted, the days continued on, and we eased into Lucy's schedule. I was getting information from Mrs. Wicks through Lucy's take-home folder, so I felt like I had a handle on her needs and schoolwork. I still hadn't received any school newsletters, but I wondered if maybe they just didn't have a reason to send one. My naivete carried me through life until one day Lucy returned home, and in her backpack was her school photo with a purchase form. She was wearing a cheap Cat & Jack T-shirt she had long grown out of, adorned with a large pink stain under the collar that was obnoxious and resistant to stain treating. Her hair was in a messy ponytail with an oversized JoJo Siwa bow on the top of her head that appeared to be falling out. I remembered the day she wore that outfit. I tried to talk her out of wearing the T-shirt, explaining it was more of a backup play shirt rather than a shirt we wear to school, but she was insistent, and I'm one to pick my battles. Had I been aware, however, it was picture day, I would have been far more persuasive. We had a brand-new dress for such an occasion, and now the moment's gone!

"You had your school pictures?" I shouted at her through the bathroom door.

"What? No. Wait. What you mean, Mama?" she replied on the toilet.

"Did you have a picture day?"

"No."

"Well, darling, I'm looking at a picture taken of you. Did

you sit in a chair and smile at a camera and then a nice man or woman took a picture of you?"

"Oh! Yeah."

"Why didn't you tell me?"

"I don't know."

I stood near the bathroom door and blinked. I had to admit, the picture was precious, but in a "my mom didn't know it was picture day" sort of way. It could have been better. I wanted it to be better. But I let the perfect kindergarten school picture go down the babbling stream.

A few moments later, I received an email from the principal. She said she was very sorry for the inconvenience, but it appears I somehow registered Lucy during a small window when they were transitioning from the old system to the new. She asked that I register Lucy again.

"I'm not even sure how you were able to register the first time; it should have been impossible!" she wrote.

What she didn't realize was that she was talking to the woman who defies the physics of registration and lists. I make the impossible, possible. But at least this explained why I'd been so mercilessly out of the loop. Lucy was never registered, and it's all been a charade. Within a few moments, I received an email from the school office:

Hello Mrs. Thomas,

Lucy has charged $12.50 worth of milk to her student account, but unfortunately she doesn't have an account. If your family needs financial assistance, please contact our office. . . .

I clicked on her phone number and swiped out of the email.

"Hello, this is Susan," the woman answered.

"Hi there!" I said with forced cheer. "This is Anna Thomas. I just received an email that Lucy has been charging $12.50 worth of milk to a nonexistent milk account. Quick question—how is a five-year-old able to purchase milk without any money?"

"Oh, yes. Lucy! She's darling."

"Uh-huh."

"Well, I happen to also be the one at the milk line, and she's so sweet. See, she's made some friends, and she follows them into the lunch line and gets herself a milk each day."

"And she's allowed to do that without money?"

"Well, it's our policy to not deny a child food in line and then follow up with the parents afterward."

"Okay, I see," I told her. Of course, when put that way, it made sense. Although it still seemed outrageous my little Lucy could waltz into a line and ring up a tab without my having any input on the matter. "So, how do I create a food account? I'm sure information has gone out, but I haven't been getting any emails. Long story."

"Oh? I'll email you a link," she said. "You can create an account there."

Once I received the link, I created an account and put about thirty dollars on her tab to cover her secret milk runs. After submitting my order, another email came through from the principal.

"Good news, parents! Due to recent COVID relief

funding, all breakfast, lunch, and milk programs will be free for all students through the 2020–2021 school year!"

"Typical," I said, rolling my eyes. "Just typical."

"Alright, Anna, now tell us," Mrs. Aboe said with a smile, "what are the highlights of your summer?"

"Well," I said, looking at my classmates, "I spent the night at Lacy's house a lot."

"Mm-hmm," she nodded, as if that was obvious. "Anything else?"

"Well, Lacy and I went to Memphis and saw Elvis's house." Lacy nodded in recognition. I had also started my period for the first time on that trip, while chaperoned by her father Merle no less, but I'd share that information another time.

"How fun!" Mrs. Aboe said, clasping her hands. "I bet that was neat!" She looked up at the clock. "Okay, everyone, we have our morning recess in about two minutes. Go ahead and line up."

After we made a line, our class followed Mrs. Aboe outside, and I followed my friends, Brett and Mark, to the four square blocks. Brett grabbed us a ball, and soon a line formed with kids anxious for their turn. In my bright green jogging pants, I stood firmly in my square. When the ball bounced before me, I smacked it good, right into the corner of Mark's square, out of his reach. The steam from the nuclear power plant billowed behind me. I giggled joyfully. Mark got mad and huffed to the back of the line. Brett laughed at his reaction, then I laughed even more. Soon, the whole line got the giggles. Our bellies shaking, eyes watering. Mark pouting.

It sounded like childhood. Ours. Flowing, babbling downstream. Gently through time.

CHAPTER 6
Chafed Thighs

Running my first 10K (10 kilometers) was thrilling, until an elderly woman holding a gallon jug of water passed me, rather easily, at the 5K mark. She was wearing an oversized T-shirt with a cartoon crab on it that read, "Oh crab! It's Monday!" along with a pair of pleated khaki shorts. But it wasn't the casualness of her running attire that troubled me—it was her significant limp. And not that she had one, but that she had one and ran past me with ease. Every time she landed on her right foot, she'd bend down and pivot sharply to the right before popping back over to her left foot. The smooth rhythm and shift transition was hypnotizing, and as I watched her grow smaller and smaller in front of me, I wondered, *Who in their right mind holds a gallon of water on a 10K run?*

But that train of thought left me with even more questions. *Why is she so thirsty? Why is she dressed as if she's tending a garden? Was she a competitive runner as a young woman and now hops into races, casually, as if it's a trip to Walgreens?* And most importantly, *How is this real life? I've been training for this!*

Many runners report a sort of euphoric daydreaming state while running, but that's not typically my experience. Instead, my subconscious mind conjures up every injustice I've experienced since birth and lets me dole out insults I'd never say in real life. Right as my rhythmic breathing hits my ears, my mind wanders to six years prior when a Walmart cashier, who, clearly annoyed by the incessant beeping, snapped when I neglected to remove my card from the payment console. She had her hair tied up in a messy bun, but she missed a very long string of hair that laid helplessly down her back. "Ma'am, that beeping is you," she sassed. "Do you see where it says remove your card? That means *remove your card.*" Mind you, this was when credit cards had just been released with chips, and we had to learn to insert instead of swipe. It was a confusing, transitional time for us all, and I could have used a little grace.

"Um, *excuse me,*" I imagined myself saying as I thumped

down the street, "I'm not stupid, I have a master's degree." I fantasized ripping the card out, grabbing my Kotex tampons, then shouting over my shoulder, "Sassing me up with your greasy rat's tail. Check ya'self!" In reality, I sheepishly apologized, not just to her, but to the people in line behind me. But my imaginary sick burn, after the fact, satisfied me well enough, and I could put the unpleasant experience behind me.

Anyway, I was heavily engaged in one such rumination when another casual insult strolled right by me. A young man with thick eyeglasses, probably in his early twenties, waltzed past me at a good clip. Getting lapped by a young man is expected under normal circumstances, but not when he looks like he just stepped out of church. He was wearing a polo, nicely pressed jean shorts, and, to my dismay, leather loafers with tassels. Did he step out of a 10:00 a.m. service, see a race going on, and then just . . . run? *Now I know why the New York City Marathon makes you qualify first,* I thought bitterly. *Omaha's just letting people in right off the pews!*

I was so deeply offended by his ability to pass me in his leather loafers, I revved up my engines to pass him. It was clearly an unsustainable pace, my lungs burned deep, but my pride could only take so much. Unlike some of my cohorts, I had fully invested in this race. I'd trained for two months, every day, and I'm still making payments on my sleek Nike running gear. I went to an actual shoe store, where the young man watched me self-consciously do a quick jog on a treadmill (unprepared, wearing a regular bra, *thank you very much*) in front of other patrons, to find the perfect shoe for my arches and natural gait. It took all afternoon, and I left with a pair of $140 ASICS! What kind of investment had Larry Loafers made? How about Gallon Gloria? None, by the looks of it. It appears they both just hopped right in on a whim and gave it a go for fun. *And they had the audacity to pass me?* My inner thighs weren't the only things chafed raw.

To keep Larry Loafers behind me, I had to maintain a near sprint as if I were some sort of Olympic athlete. To be fair, my sprint looks like someone trying to catch their Burger King wrapper caught up in the wind, but they're only making the effort because people are watching. Still, it was hard to do, and I couldn't maintain it for long. Eventually I saw his pressed jeans come up on my right side and gently pull ahead. I'd rev up again, my lungs on fire, until I couldn't take it anymore. He'd once again gently pull ahead. Of course, he had no idea I was in a weird, ego-driven competition with him. He was just doing his thing, probably wishing he'd worn better shoes but grateful for sunshine on his lazy Sunday run. I, on the other hand, was a serious runner determined to crush his will before claiming victory.

Someone a bit more reasonable would acknowledge they had more training to do and finish the race with far less angst and competitive vigor. But I simply could not accept I was that bad of a runner. I'd been training and made noticeable improvements. I assumed experienced runners would outpace me easily, but getting lapped by a kid in pressed jean shorts and an elderly woman carrying a gallon of water was more than I could bear. Although gutted, I had no choice but to let Larry Loafers pull ahead because my body was disintegrating before my eyes. The best I could do was keep running at a pace I could handle, so I did. It was slow, but I finished, so far behind Gallon Gloria and Larry Loafers that I never saw either of them again.

The Omaha Marathon event was the perfect trial run for the half-marathon I'd be running in Las Vegas, Nevada, in a year with one of my best friends, Brady. I decided to sign up for the 10K option, which would give me the opportunity to test my skills before the big Rock 'n' Roll Marathon, but I didn't get deadly serious until four months in.

The first week I trained for the 10K was enlightening. I learned things about myself I'd rather not know. For instance, I have incredibly poor bladder and, on occasion, sphincter control. My legs and hips jiggle, but not all at once, or in sync—it's as if there are various pockets jiggling at different frequencies. Meanwhile, my overall body thumps at a rhythmic beat, one that is both soothing and depressing at the same time. Don't even get me started on my lung capacity—I was struggling worse than a heavy smoker faced with an elevator's "out of order" sign. It was disconcerting, to say the least.

I knew running would be hard, but I didn't think it would be physically debilitating and emotionally humiliating. I began, as I always do, with a heightened sense of self, underestimating the difficulty and overestimating my ability to persevere. What's worse, I truly think I look like someone on the cover of *Runner's World*. Yet as I jiggled along, feeling the occurrence of shin splints before even making it one block, I was reminded of a video I watched of a family gathering. My brother-in-law was filming my nieces and nephews playing a game in the living room, as my parents watched. I *thought* I looked really good that day. My makeup was on point, my hair had great curl, and my outfit was nice and flattering. At the end of the day, we all sat around to watch the playback of the video. I was a bit bored but otherwise enjoying myself when I saw something that rocked me to my core.

It was me, in the background. Eating chips. And dip. All by myself, in the kitchen.

I suppose if I had popped one or two chips in my mouth, this wouldn't be worth mentioning, but I was hitting the tray up hard. My legs were wide, my back completely hunched over, and my hair draped down as if I were a witch stirring over a cauldron. I scooped up huge dollops of french onion dip, opened my mouth wide like a python, then slowly wedged the chip in. Chip, after chip, after chip, interrupted only by dip landing on my shirt. This forced me to pause, wet a rag, and wipe my shirt clean. Some dollops took more elbow grease than others, but I'd go right back to the bowl in due time.

While watching the video, my family was so enchanted by the children, no one noticed me at first. But I did, and I sat in shock by what I was seeing. What I viewed on the screen certainly wasn't the reality I'd experienced. *Is that really how I look when eating chips?* I wondered. My sister snapped to and noticed me. "Look at Anna in the kitchen eating chips!" she pointed, laughing. Before long, the whole family roared. I wasn't bothered by the laughing; the visuals were hilarious. What alarmed me is that no one said, "Isn't this bizarre? In person she looks stunning, but in the video she looks like Quasimodo!" No, they didn't say that, *because that's what I look like in real life eating chips.* I've just had to accept it. For most of my teen years and adulthood, if there's a photo, usually of people smiling with their arms wrapped behind each other's backs, I'm in the background, somewhere, hovered over a chip bowl. Sometimes it's like finding Waldo, but just keep looking. You'll find me.

My point is, how I think I look doing a thing and how I actually look doing a thing are usually two different things. As I began my training program, I saw myself as a fit, cute, competitive runner, but my nausea, swollen sausage fingers, and the fact I was physically suited to be a competitive quilter rather than competitive runner, told a different story. But the damage was done. In my mind, I was a runner. Everything else, as far as I was concerned, was a lie.

The pull to run came from someplace deep, and I wasn't changing my mind. Even if the whole exercise was a waste of time. Even if I looked silly or as if I didn't belong. I told myself I wanted to simply be in the best shape of my life, but what I really wanted was to be consumed by something new. Something so challenging there wasn't room for much else. Rob and I had just experienced our first miscarriage. At eight weeks, one week before my scheduled sonogram, a debilitating migraine swelled and thumped against my temples for three long, miserable days. And at the end of the third day, I went to the bathroom and lost the baby.

My sister had experienced a couple miscarriages. Several of my friends had experienced one, in some cases multiple. I knew they were common. I knew it would be alright. I'd heal and move on. But the moment Rob and I laid eyes on the positive pregnancy test, we had a dream for who this baby would be. And when the dream died, I didn't know where to go. So, I did all I could think to do.

I laced up my new $140 ASICS and ran.

Brady said he had strep throat and didn't think he could make it to Vegas. I reached my hand through the phone and slapped him across the face. The race was in three days. I trained religiously for at least six months, registered for the event, and booked my flight plus hotel at the Tropicana. We planned to run the first day and spend the following day celebrating on the Strip before flying home. Rob and I were on an extremely tight budget as it were, and a running event in Vegas was a luxury we couldn't afford. Brady wasn't allowed to get strep throat, the flu, hemorrhoids, carjacked, or shanked. Canceling was simply not an option, and I told him as much over the phone. I'd made physical, emotional, and financial investments in this race—if I wanted to run 13.1 miles by myself, I could've run around my own neighborhood and saved the expense. As we spoke, a depressing vision of me wandering around the casinos alone with a 100 oz. margarita gave me chills. "Brady," I said, putting my mouth right up to the speaker for emphasis, "I need you to listen up and listen good. Get yourself on some antibiotics, and then get your butt—that I know hasn't been properly training for a half-marathon—on that plane."

"Right, yeah, of course. I wasn't canceling," he back-tracked through shards of glass in his throat. "I was just giving you a heads-up I might not be able to run."

Brady and I have been close since we were both resident assistants in the same complex at the University of
Nebraska–Lincoln. I knew who Brady was, but I didn't know
him well until a particular Thursday, around 10:00 p.m.,
when my friend Kristin and I were smoking clove cigarettes
behind my residence hall. As an RA, I wanted to be a good
role model, so we'd hide behind the main hall in an area surrounded by bushes. As Kristin and I took big puffs of what
smelled like an intense holiday cookie, we let out a scream
when a man emerged from the bushes. "Hey, ladies!" Brady
said, also startled but pleasantly surprised to see us. "Are
you hiding and smoking?"

We looked at our cigarettes at the end of our fingers
then back at him. "Yes?"

"Can I bum one?"

He sat down with us, and we talked until the wee hours
of the morning. Brady and I would then set smoking dates,
meeting up at our hidden little spot, covering the latest gossip and all our big dreams. Over time, Brady and I would
become the best of friends, bonding over our love for high-
end cocktails and creating a life full of random adventures.
Little did we know at the time, one of those adventures,
many years later, was committing to run a half-marathon
on the Vegas Strip.

I arrived in Vegas first and waited in my hotel room
at the Tropicana for Brady to arrive. A few hours later, he
burst through the door, upbeat and jazzy. He informed me
the antibiotics had kicked in, and he felt 100 percent but
"out of an abundance of caution" wouldn't be running the
half-marathon. My lips pursed in reflex because I suspected

his decision to bow out of the race had less to do with strep throat and more to do with the fact he hadn't run a block the entire year we were supposed to be training. At that point, I didn't care. The run was for me, Vegas was for us.

The Vegas Strip really is something at night. We made our way to Mandalay Bay near the starting line, and you could feel the electricity, zipping, connecting among us. We were told to line up in sections by running ability. The most experienced runners were at the front, with lost, drunken people wondering why the Strip was so crowded tailed at the back. Since I didn't know any of the hundreds of runners personally, I was left judging people's athleticism by their looks to find my section. *Hmmm, waifish*, I observed as a woman in front of me did some light stretching, *and expensive running gear . . . too fast.* I continued to move down the line. *Okay, let's see, this woman is wearing beat-up New Balance shoes and an oversized Tweety Bird T-shirt, and she's snacking on a bag of caramel popcorn . . . too slow.* I continued to scan until I came across a woman wearing proper training gear, yet had a body type that said to me, "I can do anything I put my mind to—wait, who brought donuts?" I figured she was my best guess and cozied up beside her. I said my goodbyes to Brady, who promised to cheer me on from the sidelines. I looked at the woman next to me. She smiled weakly to let me know she wasn't making any promises.

I put my earbuds in and set my running playlist on shuffle. "Fergalicious" pumped into my ears as my feet started moving when my section got the beep to begin. The woman next to me was shoulder to shoulder for a bit of time, then fell back and I moved ahead. Running on the

Vegas Strip felt fun and ridiculous, and after a few miles, I felt my training kick in. I wasn't moving at a record pace, but I was moving at a steady one. I felt strong, happy, and confident in my stride, and things hummed along just fine until I reached mile seven. If I were a car, lights would be popping off on the dashboard, suggesting I seriously consider pulling into an auto shop. My feet were starting to feel like cement blocks, and although I felt like I was still going at a good clip, I had a sneaking suspicion I was running in place.

As we headed off the Strip into the bleaker side of Vegas, my mood began to change. I started on top of the mountain, with upbeat, magical feelings, but I soon found my attitude on a slippery slope, sliding swiftly into snark and cynicism. The pain I felt throughout my body was making me grumpy. My feet, my back, even my arms all ached, and I feared I was one string away from getting pulled apart at the seams.

As my mind cycled through ways to weasel out of finishing, I remembered I had a GU energy gel shoved into a tiny, zippered pocket of my extremely tight compression pants. GUs are popular with long-distance runners or cyclists, intended to give you a burst of energy after prolonged physical activity. I had never tried one before but picked one up before my trip just in case. I used my teeth to rip off the top of the packet and squirted the entire thing in my mouth. I assumed I would be ingesting something similar to a thick beverage, but it was basically cement in a tube. By emptying it all in my mouth, I essentially sealed my mouth shut. When you're running, breathing heavily, and then seal your mouth shut with thick sludge, it feels a lot like drowning. Out of reflex, I threw my arms out, as if I were waving someone down. Who, I don't know, but I was losing it fast. One of my flailing arms hit a woman in the boob, and I tried to say "sorry," but my mouth wouldn't open. I'm sure she saw the terror in my eyes, but it was every woman for herself—she trotted on ahead of me, growing smaller with every step.

It seems silly now, but I really thought I could die. I zig-zagged, stopping and going, choking and chomping on the GU, trying to get it out of my mouth. I had no choice but to run to the sidelines and focus most of my heavy breathing through my nose. The GU eventually dissolved enough for air to pass through, and I was able to open my mouth, gulping in dry, crisp Vegas air. After that ridiculous affair was over, I got up and kept going as if nothing happened. What else could I do? Huff, huff, huff, I went along, having gone too far to quit and hating every minute of it.

I've long heard of runner highs, but over time I experience more of a runner's emotional crisis. My emotions were all over the place, from proud of myself to genuinely hating everyone. Most of my bad attitude was from the pain still emanating from my feet and legs. I decided to lie to myself with positive affirmations. Huff, huff, huff, I feel great. Huff, huff, huff, I run great. Huff, huff, huff, I feel good. Huff, huff, huff, I hate that man's ugly shorts.

And on and on I went, huffing and criticizing toward the finish line.

Out of nowhere, a larger-than-life form came up on my right side and pulled ahead. It was a man in four-inch plat-forms dressed like '70s Elvis. I was *absolutely* incredulous. I hoped maybe he was just some sort of weird marathon hype man, but he had a running bib pinned to his cape. A woman then flanked him on his right, also dressed like Elvis in four-inch platforms, and he yelled out to her, "Twelve miles down, we're doin' it!" as they high-fived. They both began waving at people lined up against barricades on the street. For added flair, he flicked his cape, whipping it behind him, and it snapped me in the eye. "Ouch!" I said, grabbing my face, real dramatic as if my eye fell out.

"Sorry 'bout that, little lady," he said in his best Elvis impression. He wasn't even winded! I wanted to be offended so bad. The way he made it look so easy, so fun, while I was over there melting, dribbling into the gutter. Of course, a man dressed like Elvis in four-inch platform shoes would pass me with ease. *Of course he would.* So, I just held my eye in place and kept going.

Gradually, my brain began to go into sleep mode, I think as a protective mechanism, but it awakened when I saw signs that the half-marathon runners were approaching the end, and the course was splitting for the marathon runners to continue on. As I rounded a corner, I saw the finish line and went into a full sprint to end my experience on a high note. It took less than five seconds to realize that was a huge mistake, though. "Nope, nope, nope!" I said out loud, slowing my pace to barely a jog, hobbling, wobbling, and crawling several meters to the finish line. As I crossed the threshold, a nice man threw a foil blanket over me. I shook uncontrollably, drenched in sweat and freezing cold.

I was mobbed by people and fought my way to a ledge so I could sit. I tried texting Brady my location but couldn't get a strong signal. I sat alone, inside a crowd. It was a weird feeling, knowing I was done. I'd trained for that moment, and then, suddenly, it arrived. The Rock 'n' Roll Marathon was over. There was nowhere left to run. I could stop now and dream again if I wanted.

I trembled uncontrollably under my foil blanket, but a smile spread across my face.

"Anna!" I heard Brady's voice, and when I looked up, he was right there walking toward me. I felt warmth cascade over me seeing a familiar face. "Well? How'd it go? How was it?"

I slowly got up, and he grabbed my arm to steady me. "Well, Brady, to be honest," I said leaning into him, "it sucked." He nodded, as if he knew this whole thing was kinda stupid all along. "It sucked real, real bad."

"I know," he said softly. "But it's over now." Then he wrapped his arm around me, as the mob of foil-wrapped runners encircled us, gently leading me through the crowd.

CHAPTER 7
Masterpiece

H ey, sorry to interrupt," Rob said all breathy, "but Ben's in the middle of the street in his underwear, covered in blood. Should I call 911?"

I was in a meeting with my coworker, Nelson, when Rob burst in. I narrowed my brows. "Pardon?"

The student, whom I'll call Ben, was one of our residents. I was in my midtwenties, working at California State

University, Chico, as a resident director while also getting my master's degree. Nelson and I supervised the RAs at our complex and managed student conduct, buildings, and events. I had a separate apartment on campus where Rob and I lived together. He was on his way to work when he saw him in the street.

Ben had Asperger's syndrome—a form of autism that affects the ability to effectively socialize and communicate. I guess you could say that Ben could be, a little, socially awkward, but delightful in his own sweet ways. He would visit my office every morning and chat away about his favorite things. Our conversations were usually technical and in great detail, so I would try in earnest to stay present. Inevitably, my mind wandered toward which RA I could talk into getting me a Starbucks. When it had gone on a bit too long, I'd have to gently usher him out my door so I could finally take a few personal calls in my office.

Ben was gentle and kind. He could be counted on to attend all our resident events. This endeared me to him because sometimes he'd be the only one there. For an RA who was already terrified no one would show up to their "Saved by the Bell" dance party, he'd be there in the corner with his black biker jacket, drinking punch. (I think he was supposed to be Tori Scott, Zack Morris's love interest in the last season?) He was a beloved fixture in our little community.

I shot a look at Nelson to get his vibes on the bloody-kid-in-the-middle-of-the-street situation, and he waved me off to let me take care of it. Nelson grew up in Colombia and had this "I've seen everything" way about him.

I ran out of the office and gave Rob the okay to head to work. I looked out to the main road outside our complex, where Ben was, indeed, just standing there in the middle of the road, wearing only his tighty-whities, covered in blood. It was hard to process what I was looking at and why I was looking at it. *Had he been beaten up? Was this his blood? Is this someone else's blood? On no, he killed somebody,* I decided. *I don't have time for this.*

Emily did something pretty stupid, but that's par for the course when drinking a bottle of Sailor Jerry. It was late on a Friday night, and she had a few friends in her dorm room. As people often do when buzzed, especially me, they laughed too loudly during quiet hours. The RAs on duty knocked, and after lots of shushing behind the door, Emily opened it, with an obviously fake calm and collectedness drunk people do when they're pretending to be calm and collected. The bottle of Sailor Jerry rum was on the table behind her in plain view. The RAs wrote her up, and now she had to see me.

"This doesn't seem like you, Emily," I said, pulling up the report on my computer. It felt odd, pretending to be the kind of professional person who "pulls reports." I was in my midtwenties, and certainly an adult, but I totally believed the scientists who claim our brains don't fully develop until age twenty-five. It was as if my brain had just finally closed its most immature gaps and was now looking around, thinking, *I don't have to start paying for my own insurance now, do I?*

Emily was a good student who stayed out of trouble. The whole debacle seemed out of character but even more so since she didn't even bother to hide the evidence.

"I know," she said. "I don't know what I was thinking."

Her case was pretty straightforward. After we discussed what happened, I scheduled a meeting for her on campus, where she'd receive her official disciplinary notice, little more than a slap on the wrist for the first offense.

"How's everything going?" I asked. "Are you making friends? Having fun? Learning?" I barely recognized myself. Who did I think I was, pretending to be some kind of adult mentor, in a NY&C stretch blazer and stretchy slacks that were essentially glorified yoga pants? And yet I had my own office, and when students sat across from me, they were nervous. Frankly, it was ludicrous.

To be honest, I felt more like a child putting on a play of what they thought an adult would do or say. At the time, Rob and I were in early marriage counseling with his pastor, and that alone felt like peak adulting. It was our way of getting our marriage off on the right foot, and my way of fleshing out everything that bothered me about Rob so he could fix it as soon as possible. During one session, Rob and I were going back and forth about something dumb and petty. I don't remember what we were going on about, but I do remember what our pastor said: "You two should go out and volunteer somewhere. Go to a soup kitchen and serve folks a meal. Just do something for someone else and stop thinking about yourselves." I squirmed on the couch. Rob and I were gently touching fingers and, once convicted, subtly withdrew them. "It'll remind you the world doesn't revolve around you." Then he looked at his watch and back at us. "It'll be good for you."

I wanted to be offended, but I had to admit he had a point. All I really thought about was me and my feelings about things. My career. My marriage. My life's "purpose," even though I didn't really know what that meant. I believed everyone's ultimate mission in life was finding their purpose, and it was supposed to be epic. But as I was gradually exposed to common human heartaches and suffering, I grew afraid. I feared an artist isn't living out her divine purpose when she puts paint to canvas and creates a masterpiece. When it gets featured in galleries, praised and admired. I feared a true masterpiece is to sit with someone as they grieve, helping a stranger with their heavy groceries, or offering to watch a single mom's toddler so she can mosey through Target, alone. This, of course, is far less exciting. There aren't many accolades, awards, or prizes for these types of things. Most of my twenties up until that point was playing the part, self-absorbed and oblivious to the fact that I'm not really that special. I felt hurt when the realization cascaded over me, but when the pastor dismissed my pettiness, I also felt relieved.

Emily didn't appear scared or worried like a lot of students were when they sat across from me at my desk, but she did seem distracted. "Yeah, things are fine," she said. "School is great, my friends are great."

"Oh, I'm so glad. And you like your major?"

She shifted in her seat. "Can we not talk about this?"

"Oh. *Okay.*" I was a bit miffed but tempered it so she

wouldn't notice. "Sure. Of course. You're free to go, your appointment on campus is Tuesday at 10:00 a.m."

"No, sorry, I didn't mean that," she stammered. "I don't want to leave. I just want to talk about something else."

My brows furrowed. I sensed it was about to get serious, and I was tempted to lift my finger for a brief pause so I could get my mom on speaker. Mom has always known what to do, especially in the realm of helping or counseling women, since it's something she's done for most of her adult life. I haven't always been codependent with my mom, but I have been needy much of the time. The natural progression for many children of loving parents is to be dependent as a child, then instinctively set sail during emerging adulthood in order to prove to ourselves, and them, we're grown. Then, as a handful of years go by and we realize we're grown, but clueless, we begin to wash back onto our parents' shore, with a new desire to share our adulthood with them, savoring their wisdom.

But I must say, as I've gotten older, there were several times when calling Mom in the midst of a crisis, or in need of good advice, I could tell she was just making stuff up. Especially if I interrupted an episode of her favorite TV show. One time I bit into a scorching hot brat, and the juice burned my lip so bad it was like I had a canker sore from hell on my lip. "Pierce a vitamin E capsule and put it directly on your lip; should clear it right up by tomorrow," she said with confidence. I was so full of hope and desperate to get the massive blister off my face, I left immediately to the nearest health food store to find top-of-the-line vitamin E capsules to heal me quick.

"So just put it right on the burn?" I asked, calling her from the car.

"Yeah, you know what? I have no idea if that'll work, you better google it," she said, ushering me off the phone. "Your father and I are in the middle of *Doc Martin*, and he's staring at me. Let's talk later." Frustrated and feeling slightly betrayed, I headed off to a social justice training on campus, and the only seat left was next to the facilitator. I sat there, my lower lip enlarged beyond recognition, blistered, and now covered in thick vitamin E goop. "My apologies for the distracting debacle on my face," I said sheepishly. "I burned my lip on a brat."

"Oh, I didn't even notice," she said politely. But what else is a social justice facilitator going to say? My coworker chimed in, "Oh, that's a burn? I thought you had some kind of nasty canker sore." And his frank response felt closer to the truth.

So, while my mom's halfhearted advice happened often enough to give me some pause, she was usually on point and, bottom line, my only hope. Yet, as Emily started going off script, I knew getting my mom on speaker was probably a bad look. I was a professional, whether I liked it or not, and should suck it up and hope for the best.

"I'm, I'm, um," she looked around my office and fixated on a poster of an Andy Warhol painting of a banana. In fact, most of my students would fixate on the poster in a curious way. Over time, I became insecure that perhaps it was a phallic symbol of some sort, and I was either the house mom who didn't get it or the incredibly inappropriate resident director with a phallic symbol in her office. I nodded again and smiled for her to finish her sentence.

"I'm gay." The room stood still for just a moment, then she burst into tears. And she did it in a way that was so tender and raw, it made my eyes well up too. But she didn't hide her face, as people often do. Grief can be so private and, in front of others, feel embarrassing. But she just looked right at me and cried.

"Oh my," I said, softly. I grabbed a tissue off my desk and handed it to her. "Is this the first time you've shared this?"

"No, I told my roommate."

"And? How did she respond?"

"Happy, supportive. She's cool."

"Have you told your parents?"

"Not yet," she said, blowing hard into the tissue. I handed her another.

"And how do you think they'll take the news?"

"I think they'll take it fine," she muttered. Then she got to weeping again, "I'm not worried about that."

I adjusted and squeaked in my chair, trying to figure out what exactly the problem was. Not to minimize the depth of her pain, but I couldn't figure out why she felt the need to burst such a private dilemma out into the open, with me of all people, as she was written up for a bottle of Sailor Jerry. But as she continued to cry, I grasped at any floating wisp of job training I could find twirling to the surface. Like a counselor, my job wasn't to offer my perspective, cast judgments, or include myself at all. I just needed to be safe, a storm shelter until the pounding emotions quieted and she could go back outside. As time went on, sitting quietly together, it seemed her sobs weren't rooted in fear of how those closest to her would react. And she wasn't looking for advice. Instead, it seemed as if she simply needed a room, a room with someone in it, to cry in.

My right leg had been crossed awkwardly during our meeting, and my foot was dead asleep. The tingly phase had long passed while I was distracted and had moved into the possible amputation phase. But how could I not get up and give her a hug? As I rose, I held out my arms, gesturing with the "bring it in" motion. Sadly, as I did so, it was painfully obvious my foot was practically decomposing and needed to be removed. As we both took steps toward each other for a hug, my entire leg gave out, causing me to crash into her aggressively. It was still technically a hug, but more so one person trying to hold another person up. Instead of sharing a quiet moment together, I had to stomp my foot into the ground repeatedly to get some sort of sensation to return.

"Thank you for trusting me with your heart," I said, now thumping my foot against my metal desk. "Come back and see me, not because you're drinking in your room, but to say hi. Okay?"

"Okay," she said, making her way to my office door. "Thank you."

"You're welcome." I smiled back, lifting my foot in the air like an injured bird.

She lingered there for a few more moments, before leaving and shutting the door behind her. After that day, she never had to see me because of Sailor Jerry. And she never stopped again to say hi.

My first semester at the University of Nebraska–Lincoln, I roomed with my "best friend" from high school. But Ava and I were never truly close. We hung out a lot and had fun, but it was as if we had given each other the label as a form of social currency, a way for us to claim a special bond and be exclusive among our circle of friends. She was popular, and I could be, too, by proxy. I was the funny girl, and she could be the funny girl's closest friend.

I knew it was a mistake to live with her but figured it was better to live with the devil I knew. She was mean in high school, and I braced myself for what living with her might be like. She wasn't all bad, of course. Few people really are. Most of the time she was charming, caring, and funny.

But in the shadows, she was mean. One wrong move and she'd cut you off and ice you out. We shared the same friend group, and the way she'd so publicly rebuff me was embarrassing. Looking back, I assume she had deep-rooted emotional issues, because only a child inherently hurting would have acted that way. And only a child, inherently insecure, would have put up with it. I'm embarrassed to admit, I did for a long time.

On a mundane Wednesday morning, Ava announced she was moving out at the end of the semester with a new best friend she met on our floor. And she was unnecessarily cold about it too. My heart broke. I was young for my class, still just seventeen, and it was my first semester away from home. I felt so rejected and alone, I couldn't bear to sit in our room anymore. I got up to leave, and the only place I could think to go was Jamie's room. She was a junior RA, living in a residence hall nearby. I met her at a Bible study, and she invited me and a few others to walk with her to football games or hang out at campus events. I knocked on Jamie's door, relieved when she opened it. She had a big smile on her face that fell when she saw I wasn't quite myself.

"Hey, can we talk?" I asked her. Concerned, she brought me to her futon to sit. "I like your room," I said, fidgety, beginning to regret the whole thing. She barely knew me, and there I was so fragile and weepy.

"Oh, thanks," she shrugged and smiled, nodding slowly, waiting for me to get to the point.

After a few more awkward pauses, I shook loose and told her everything. She gave me a big hug and smelled soft, like vanilla. I cried on her shoulder for a long time. Perhaps, awkwardly long, but Jamie didn't make me feel that way. And while Ava's rejection led the emotional brigade, the length of my tears was to release the insecure teenage girl who allowed a friend to treat her like trash. I knew I was better than that. And I knew I deserved better. I grieved the loss of a friendship, but mostly I grieved the part of me I was anxious to leave behind.

Jamie was wearing a light blue T-shirt, and I sobbed into her right shoulder. After several long minutes, I lifted my head from her shoulder and, to my horror, left a plate-sized wet spot, covered in mascara and snot.

"Oh no, I stained your shirt," I said, pointing at her shoulder.

"Oh, it's okay," she said, her neck tilted down trying to get a good view of it. "That's what laundry detergent is for."

"It's waterproof mascara, so, maybe um, use a little

Shout," I meekly suggested. Jamie said very little during the time I was there, nor did I want her to, as we sat together in the quiet of her room. She invited me to stay for as long as I needed, and when she sensed I was all cried out, she changed her shirt and sat on the couch with me while she did her homework. We sat together quietly while I let my mind wander and gather its courage to go back to my room. She had a huge Dave Matthews poster on her wall. I gazed at it for about twenty minutes before deciding it was time to leave.

"Thank you, I should go now," I said, brushing down my shirt. She rose from the futon and gave me another big hug. I walked to her door and lingered. "Thanks again."

"Come back anytime to hang out or just say hi," she said, and I believe she meant it. I assured her I would, and I believe I meant it too. But as Ava moved out, Carmen moved in, and I moved on—I never made the time, for reasons I can't fully explain, to stop by. Or even say hi again.

Ben was standing on a center island as cars zoomed by in both directions. As the cars cleared, I ran to him and met him at the island.

"I, I, I'm so sorry. I don't know what I'm doing," he said as I approached him.

"Do you recognize me, Ben?" I tried to comfort him and looked for a patch of peach skin I could pat that wasn't covered in sticky dark red.

"Yes, you're Anna."

"Let's get out of the road, okay? It's not safe here." We waited until cars cleared again and ran swiftly to the sidewalk. I stopped to call 911, holding him by his elbow.

"Do you recognize this place? Where you are?" I asked him after I got off the phone.

"I'm on campus," he muttered.

"Good! That's right. Do you know you were in the middle of the street, and why you're bleeding so badly?" At this point, I was just winging it. Of course, my coworkers and I went through rigorous training. Since we lived among the students, we were typically at the scene first for any crisis, like water geysers coming from sprinklers, assaults, overdoses, and medical emergencies. But unfortunately, I was barely paying attention during most of the training, daydreaming about what I wanted for lunch, the state of my nails, or a curiosity about a coworker's dead tooth.

"No. I, I, I don't know what I'm doing." Ben was scared, speaking and acting like someone who closed their eyes and then woke up in an alternate universe. We walked slowly back to his room. Our complex has many older residents and was set up more like an interconnected complex than a typical dorm. We stopped when we stumbled upon our first clue.

"Well, I think we know why you're so bloody," I told him, moving forward to get a closer look. The entire bay window to his room was busted out, with jagged shards of glass jutting out the frame.

"Too good to exit through a door like the rest of us idiots, *amirite Ben?*" I said, easing into a chuckle that I quickly phased out. I have a tendency to try and make people laugh in the midst of little traumas to ease the tension, but it usually backfires. In high school, my friend took a turn too fast on fresh asphalt and rear-ended an elderly couple. As the police pulled up, I opened the passenger door and flopped out like a dead body. It's a coping mechanism, don't overthink it.

We were careful to avoid glass as we made our way into his room. I had a small pack of tissues in my back pocket I'd stolen from the main housing office and used one to help get blood out of his eyes. I inspected his cuts and tried to act like an adult by keeping a confident look on my face. I'd never seen that much blood. I think the last time anything ever came close was when my mom cut her hand dicing an onion, and as I recall, I screamed, ran into my room, locked the door, and put a pillow over my head.

Some of his cuts had clotted and stopped running. A few, particularly on his legs and hands, were very deep, but none of them were bleeding in a "Let me tear off my shirt and make a tourniquet!" sort of way, and for that I was grateful because I wasn't wearing my good bra.

He was apologizing before getting interrupted by sirens. I told Ben to sit on his chair (and stay there!) so I could greet them and bring them back to his room to help us. I gave two policemen the rundown, and when we got back to Ben's room, they immediately took over.

After asking a few questions, they surmised Ben was on a new medication and woke in a sleepwalking state. He busted out his windows with his fists, hoisted his gangly legs over the edge, and wound up in the middle of the street. I mean, he broke out a bay window with those little chicken wings? Good grief, humans really can do whatever we set our minds to.

They left the room and made the call for paramedics to arrive. I was helping Ben find a comfortable pair of shorts when my phone made a ding; I was late for a meeting.

"You can go," Ben said, looking in my direction, his eyes low.

"No, I'm going to cancel," I said. "I'd like to stay if that's alright with you?"

"Yeah," he said, flashing the tiniest little smile.

Ben's room was plain, a little messy, but tidier and less smelly than what you'd imagine for a typical college boy's room. "I like what you've done with the place," I said, trying to fill the empty space.

"Thank you. I'm pretty good at decorating."

"I can tell." I noticed he was trembling. Probably scared and cold, worried about what he'd done. I cleared my throat. "You know what impresses me most about you?" I asked him. He shoved his glasses up his nose and looked at me. "How strong you are, busting through the window like that."

"Um, yeah. I curl those weights every day." He lifted his long, thin arm and pointed at a couple of five-pound weights sitting on the floor by his desk.

"I guess so! There's no way I'm strong enough to break a window. I'm impressed." We smiled at each other. Nelson had arrived by then, standing outside talking to the police officers.

Ben and I sat on his unmade bed. We listened as men spoke in hushed tones, as students walked by, laughing and hollering, swirling around outside as they tend to do. But inside, we were still, like a painting. Two people, in a little room, a little scared, with shards of glass twinkling around them like diamonds. Waiting quietly inside our own little masterpiece.

Then we heard it. Off in the distance, the faint sound of an ambulance siren making its way toward us. "Here they come," I said, patting his knee. We listened together, intently. Louder and louder, the siren grew, whooping, high pitched. Looking for us. Closer, closer, closer.

CHAPTER 8
Terror in the Closet

I was standing there in the closet, like an idiot. It was dark, cramped, and my breath made it sticky and humid. Anxiety vibrated throughout my body. The walls seemed to cave in, smothering me in winter coats. The only light I could see came through the slight crack of the closet's door, where I could see a man standing outside.

My heart was pounding inside my ears. My breath

shallow, afraid to make a sound. I forced myself to breathe in, slowly, quietly, but deeply. Then I exhaled, easing air through my lips. My eye pressed to the crack, I could see his figure, slowly opening the sliding glass door.

I prepared for this moment and already had the lights off, the apartment lit by only moonlight and a streetlight outside our window. This was a long time coming. Rob and I were freshly married, and throughout most of our marriage, he would entertain himself by sneaking into the house while I was unaware, then jump out behind doors, shower curtains, beds, and so on, in order to scare me to within an inch of my short, miserable life.

And it didn't matter how mad it made me, how seriously I threatened him, or the one time I shuffled through kitchen drawers for a carving knife, he would laugh and laugh and laugh and never stop because my "hilarious" scream and apparent terror made it worth the risk.

To make it worse, he would often scare me while I was in the middle of something private, like the one time I was multitasking by going to the bathroom and trimming my toenails at the same time, with my foot hoisted up on my knee like some kind of barbarian. Rob gingerly opened the door to our home, crept in like a criminal, tiptoed in the house, then burst into the bathroom so that for a brief moment, I'd fear my life ending. I screamed my terror scream, and those who know me well know it's not so much your typical high-pitched movie scream but more like Joan Rivers and James Earl Jones trying to sing *a capella*. He scared me so deeply, I got up to run but tripped because my pants were around my ankles. I crashed headfirst into the wall and then slowly slid down, losing my dignity with every slithery inch.

To say he almost died that day at the bare hands of his wife is an understatement. I was thirsty for revenge.

Rob's predictable schedule played to my advantage. His shift ended at 8:00 p.m., and he always walked through the door at 8:11 p.m., right to the second. At 7:45 p.m., I waited on the couch alone, quietly preparing myself for what I had to do. At 8:00 p.m., I got up and set the stage for my attack. I turned off the lights and made my way into the closet. Although I was nervous, I moved methodically like a woman who made up her mind and there was no turning back. I propped the closet door open just enough that I got a view of our sliding glass door—the door off our patio that he always used to get into our apartment. He'd texted earlier, and I knew he had a difficult day. I assumed he'd be exhausted, vulnerable, and ill-equipped to handle his wife jumping out of a closet to terrify him. As I stood alone in a cramped coat closet like a moron, I felt a deep sense of vindication and satisfaction by the mere thought of enacting my revenge.

In retrospect, I probably didn't need ten minutes of "prep" time to flip a light switch off and slip into a closet. That's a long time to be flooded with strange, zingy feelings of terror and anticipation, as if I were on a roller coaster about to head over the cliff. A few times, I lost my nerve and almost got out to relax and watch Food Network. But I knew that if I didn't give Rob what he deserved, which was cold-blooded, jump-out-of-the-closet revenge, he'd never stop scaring me.

It was time.

My brother screamed a lot when I was little, and it's probably because my dad liked to jump out of closets. Christian is five years older, and both of us were scaredy-cats all through elementary school, needing our dad to lie with us in bed until we fell asleep. First it was my brother, then I followed suit. For nearly a decade, Dad was forced to spend his first couple hours of sleep on the uncomfortable mattress of a child's bed. I remember one evening, the summer before fifth grade, my mom tried to break the cycle. A rerun of *Walker, Texas Ranger* had just ended, our cue to head on up to bed. "Anna, sweetheart?" my mom said gently, sitting stoically in a wingback chair. "Do you think Daddy could sleep with me tonight? You're a big girl. Why don't you try falling asleep by yourself for a little while?" I should have been ticked by her selfishness, the sheer audacity of it, but I wasn't even trying to take her seriously.

I turned to my dad and scoffed. "You hear this woman?" I said, rolling my eyes. "Come on, Daddy, let's go." My poor father, who was incapable of saying no to any child, and to this day still suffers at their whims, shrugged at my mom and followed me up to my room, where he would lie next to me until he could hear the soft, rhythmic breathing of a sleeping child. When that would be, exactly, was anyone's guess. Ten minutes? Two hours? One time I was just about to slip into sleep when I was jolted awake by the feeling of his weight lifting off the mattress. "Where do you think you're going?" I asked, my arm propped against my pillow. I could see his shoulders sink in the moonlight before he lay back down. "Alright, Annie," he said, as I wrapped my arm around him, cuddling him tight like a teddy bear.

I don't think the Beav's father in *Leave It to Beaver* jumped out of closets to scare his children, but Dad was still a man of traditional family values. He wouldn't dream of scaring me or my sister. We were girls, young women to protect. Christian, on the other hand, was fair game. It was just part of becoming a man, I suppose, even if my dad had to then assist him in falling asleep shortly after. What made this scare particularly egregious was the great length Dad went toward setting its stage. A person who lives with a prankster can often sense when the energy has shifted. The air becomes dense, something feels amiss. If they're lucky, they get ahead of the prankster and thwart their efforts. In fact, a few times Christian was able to do just that. "Dad," he'd say, lying on the couch, watching TV. "I know you're hiding behind the chair. I can see your white Reeboks." My dad would then shimmy out from behind the chair, smooth his shirt, and head to work. The only trouble is, catching pranksters in the act only strengthens their resolve. They become more determined and creative. Some will even wait it out, going weeks or even months, making you think they've grown bored of scaring you. Then *bam*! Your life flashes before your eyes. It's sick is what it is.

I was about five or six years old, drifting to sleep in my parents' bed, when I heard a bloodcurdling scream. It was followed by thumping and pounding sounds as my brother flew down the stairs. I've always seen my brother as a strong, strapping man, even when we were little, so I was terrified to hear him scream like Marion Crane in *Psycho*. I sat up on alert trying to parse out sounds but relaxed once I heard my dad's low, rhythmic, guffaw laugh billowing throughout the entire home. *Oh good, Daddy's just scaring Christian again*, I thought, yawning as I laid my head back against the pillow. My mom was downstairs, sweeping up the night's final crumbs off the kitchen floor, when Christian came barreling in toward her. "Richard!" Mom screamed from downstairs. "You've scared him half to death!" My dad began wheezing, his laugh now coming down deep from his lungs instead of his throat. He was still at the top of the steps, his body convulsing too much to safely make it down. For at least five minutes, he was just wheezing and throwing out words, "You should have seen," wheeze, wheeze, wheeze, "his face," wheeze, wheeze, wheeze, "he thought I was in bed," wheeze, wheeze, wheeze, "towels!" Then my dad took in big gulps of air, trying not to pass out.

While Christian was in the bathroom brushing his teeth, Dad had taken towels out of the linen closet, and on his side of the bed, formed the shape of a body. He covered the towels with the bed's comforter, before slipping inside Christian's bedroom closet. My brother walked in, sat on the edge of his bed to take off his socks, and started chatting with the towel form he thought was his loving, protector father. When Dad burst from the closet, Christian took off as if his butt were on an ocean wave of terror, giving my dad one of the purist delights of his life.

If you were to ask my dad about it now, he'd say he has regrets. Sure, we still laugh real hard about it, but it doesn't stop him from feeling remorse. "Poor boy was scared to sleep as it was," he said after it got brought up at a recent family dinner. "Hurts my heart to think about me scaring him like that." Dad has softened as he has grown into a grandpa, regretting some of his antics as a young father. Christian, now a large brute of a man, doesn't feel a need for sympathy. "What?" he scoffed, before taking a bite of a brat. "It's fine, Dad, it was funny." But you have to wonder, *are you sure?*

I've heard it said that women often end up marrying a man like their dad, but this isn't my experience. My husband, Rob, shares only three characteristics with my own father—the two I value most—he's a family man with a really good sense of humor. But remove those two pillars, and everything else about their careers, personalities, and even hobbies is the exact opposite. My mom and I processed this on a drive together right after I was married. Why wasn't I drawn to men more like my father? Then it struck me, "Mom, I didn't marry a man like Dad because . . . *I am* Dad." Mom's eyes grew wide in recognition before slapping her knee, "Oh, Anna! You're right!"

And these are the kinds of things you think about alone, in a dark closet. Standing there, with bated breath, just like my father all those years ago. I wanted, no I needed, this scare to be so good, so legendary, someone would write it down in a book. Recorded in history, passed down generation to generation. If I had to be the one to write, so be it.

Time really moves slowly when you're standing in a dark

closet trying to scare your husband. But when I heard the gate close, I snapped to attention. My heart flew right off the road, like a tire falling off a truck going 100 miles per hour. If Rob detected me, in any way, it was over. My hands shook as I tried to control my breaths. I watched his body approach the sliding glass door. But then something unexpected happened—he stopped.

What is he doing? I wondered. He was looking through the window, scanning up and down, looking for something, but what could it be?

Me.

This idiot was trying to scare me again!

Ever so delicately, he grabbed the door handle and slowly slid it open. The deliciousness of the moment made me flush and nearly faint. Scaring him while he's trying to scare me would be the ultimate revenge. Failure was not an option, but I really had to get it together. I grew lightheaded from the smothering closet and my rapidly rising heartbeat. I kept my eye to the crack and watched him slowly open the door, step delicately inside, then slowly close it, being ever so precious as he let it click.

He dropped his backpack softly, then crept slowly toward me. My guess was he was going to head down the hall, assuming I was in our bedroom. I had to time my scare just right. Open the door too soon before he gets to me and I'll startle him, but not terrorize him—the entire point of this exercise. Wait too long, and he'll be past me, causing the same effect. I needed to burst out at him at just the right moment so he'd genuinely fear for his life. It would be my most glorious, crowning achievement. *Feet don't fail me now!*

I held my breath. Seconds felt like minutes. Then, ready or not, he stepped in just the right spot. I closed my eyes tight, then boom! I exploded from the closet.

"Boo!" I screamed, guttural and primal, kicking the closet door wide open. The door missed him by centimeters, my body flung at him with boo scare hands. He screamed, and the shrill, reverberating sound was better than anything I could have possibly imagined! It was girly, bloodcurdling, and deeply, *deeply* satisfying. His eyes grew wide, and I saw pure fear twirling, bouncing around inside. It was just a millisecond, but pure satisfaction flooded my body as it responded to the delightful sounds and sights of his terror. My rapture was short-lived, however, when his arm cocked back and he punched at my face. It happened so quickly, there was no time to mentally ingest what was happening. From pure biological, survival instinct, I moved my head out of the way of his fist, á la *The Matrix*, slow motion and real badass, while his fist whooshed past my face and punched the door. I swung around just in time to see his hand punch halfway through it.

"My hand!" he screamed, clutching it with his left hand.

"Hahahahahahaha! Sucka!" I roared with laughter. With my finger pointing at him, I shouted, "I got you bad! And you scream like a girl!"

"Why would you do that?" he cried. He removed his hand, revealing dark red blood, smeared and pouring from an open gash, "My god, I'm bleeding!"

"Hahahahahaha!" I continued on in pure delight. "Wait, what? Like bad? Are you bleeding bad?"

Oh great, this was a real buzzkill. I grew deeply annoyed

as it bled at a pretty good clip. "You should get a Band-Aid on that," I said. Desperate to not lose the moment, I added, "But did you see how I scared you? And like, you screamed all high-pitched and hilarious? And you almost punched me square in the face, but I sidestepped it like this." I reenacted the moment, leaning back and swishing my head around real slick. He moved past me, bumping my shoulder still gliding in slow motion, to wash his wound at the sink. It was official—his cut was stealing my thunder. "I mean, I got ya real good, didn't I? And the best part? You were trying to scare me! Oh, it feels so good!" The moment was far too delicious, I had to fight for my joy. I simply could not let his injury rain on my parade.

"Yep, you got me," he said back, wincing as the water flushed through his wound, "and that door's gonna be expensive to replace." One can only experience joy for so long in the face of someone's blood, tears, and budget concerns. My rush of good feelings was turning into a dribble. Eventually all I could do was stand there with my hands on my hips, utterly dejected. I had finally landed my first epic revenge scare, and now I have to feel bad about a bloodied wound? And the cost of a new door?

Nope, not today! I stayed strong. He made his bed, now lie in it!

I continued to brag, poke, and prod, but I could tell it hurt, and he was upset. It was inevitable, the air had no choice but to seep out of the balloon. What else could I do but postpone my gloating and give him a little space? Slowly, he managed to clean his wound (I've cut myself worse shaving my legs, can we move on?), bandage it, get out of his scrubs, and make his way to the couch to watch a little TV. I sat next to him and cozied up.

"Babe?" I said.

"Yes?" he replied.

"What do you think hurts worse right now? Your hand or your pride?"

"My pride," he said, changing the channel. "Definitely my pride." He smirked. Just a little. It was the teensiest affirmation, but it was enough. He never scared me again.

Sometimes I wonder if, like my dad, I too will regret going a bit too far. After all, his hand still has a visible, jagged scar.

Eh, I doubt it.

CHAPTER 9
Bossy

Within hours of bringing my husband home from his vasectomy, I caught him on the couch with a pack of organic Cascadian Farm California-style blend halfway down his pants.

"Why aren't you using an ice pack?" I snipped. I had a basket of dirty laundry on my hip; this was the last thing I needed.

"Frozen vegetables mold better."

"Hmm, interesting," I said. "Had I been properly warned that frozen vegetables were preferred to ice packs, I would have purchased the cheap GMO corn." Not only were those organic frozen vegetables expensive, it was the side dish for the chicken dinner I had planned for later that evening.

"We can still eat this. The bag is sealed," he muttered, grimacing.

"No one's eating thawed vasectomy vegetables," I snapped, turning with a huff to the laundry room.

I knew I was in for the long haul when Rob hobbled pitifully out of the clinic like Tiny Tim. Even I'll admit, he really took one for the team by volunteering to get snipped, but I sensed early on he was going to lean in hard to his sacrifice. He was a nurse, working as a case manager in cardiology. Like most in a medical profession, he'd seen a lot, so he wasn't initially squeamish about getting a vasectomy. Yet, although it sounded good on paper, one can't underestimate the emotional attachment men have to their wieners. He's like a soldier, constantly on guard, protecting his king. Truth is, I can't even flap a piece of cardboard near his parts without the stiff breeze causing him to scream like the woman in *King Kong*. So, I should have known, despite his initial cavalier attitude, perhaps we'd both bitten off more than we could chew.

I was drinking a Route 44 Strawberry Limeade from a Sonic fast-food restaurant when the nurse called to tell me I had gestational diabetes. Bewildered and offended, I curtly replied, "I'm sorry, this is Anna Thomas—I think you've dialed the wrong number," and hung up.

It shouldn't have been such a shocking and devastating diagnosis. Poppy was a larger baby, and I carried a lot of extra amniotic fluid during the pregnancy. Plus, I was thirty-six. In pregnancy years, it meant I should be yelling out "bingo!" in a nursing home. But it still made me feel like a failure, as if I'd done something wrong. That perhaps my oddly specific obsession to Route 44 Strawberry Limeades and Cheesecake Factory french fries had given my baby a hostile dump to grow in rather than the luxury womb rich celebrities give their children.

After the diagnosis, I was told I needed to attend a nutrition class to help manage my blood sugar. Without question, the class was a positive, and a necessity to help pregnant women manage their blood sugar safely. But whatever, I was ticked. Defensive. Brimming with pride and arrogance. *Did they even know my mother?* She was fighting against the dangers of sugar and white flour back when nutritionists were approving Lucky Charms as a healthy, low-fat meal for kids. And she paid the price too—she was a pariah, a social outcast. And so was I, by proxy. At school, we were having a food drive of some sort, and I was tasked with bringing a box of Jell-O. Puzzled, I raised my hand. "Excuse me, but what's Jell-O?" The whole class looked at me like I was a freak.

My mom's obsession with proper nutrition and using food to heal began when my brother, just a toddler, became deathly ill with whooping cough. She spent many days in the hospital and countless hours rocking him on a toilet, the hot steam of her shower filling the room while he gasped and wheezed. The more she learned about food before humans got our prickly little chemistry lab fingers all over it, the more disgusted she became. Because of this, I grew up believing the government guidance many nutritionists followed was pure nonsense. And, at least during my formative years, it was. Remember when eggs were demonized, but margarine and fat-free Twinkies were on the food pyramid? And these fools were going to teach *me* how to eat healthy? It's like my mother was Meryl Streep, and I was forced to take acting lessons from Beverly at the community youth center. I mean, *please.*

"My number was off by one. I probably don't even have it," I told my nurse practitioner. I'd been edgy all morning anticipating the appointment and was now sitting before her with the pregnancy sweats. The crinkly paper on the exam table stuck to the back of my thighs, and I was skating the razor's edge of an emotional breakdown. "I don't need someone to teach me how to eat healthy. I know how this crap works; they're gonna recommend Diet Pepsi and sugar-free jelly on my peanut butter sandwiches. The whole thing's a joke."

Throughout my pregnancies with both girls, my nurse practitioner was encouraging and compassionate. But on that particular day, she wasn't feeling it. "Anna, they're going to teach you how to monitor and manage your blood sugar, okay? It's very important you go," she said, ushering me to lie down on the exam table. "Gestational diabetes can be managed safely, but you need to learn how, or it can be very dangerous for the baby."

"But I don't have it."

"And if you refuse to go," she continued, "our clinic can no longer see you as a patient."

Wow. Just—wow. *Now she's threatening me?* my mind spun. *What is this, North Korea? I have rights!*

I was so frustrated and angry and full of myself. My emotions were a slurry of shame and fear—resistance to my reality and resistance to being controlled. I burst into tears, my pregnancy hormones like a NASCAR race, cars colliding, flipping in the air, catching on fire.

"I don't want to go," I wailed, "and I don't need to go!" Was all this drama really necessary? All I had to do was go to a brief, informative class, but I was acting like an innocent woman sentenced to life without parole.

"Hormones at this stage of pregnancy can be very powerful," she said quietly. I stopped sobbing to shoot a few eye darts at her, then lay back down on the exam table so she could gently push and feel my belly. I cried, audibly, during her entire exam. Normally, crying over something so stupid in front of a non–family member would have been humiliating, but my pregnancy hormones were like an alternate personality. A sassy, wild, and dangerous personality whom I called Tina. She was cozied next to me, stroking my sweaty hair from my forehead, cooing in my ear. "Of course, you're upset. These idiots can't force us to do anything," she whispered. "They're not the boss of us." Tears poured down my cheeks as I nodded in agreement. Tina was so right. No one was gonna make me take some stupid class I didn't need for some condition I didn't even have.

I'm the boss.

After my fifth wrong turn to the gestational diabetes class, I'd about had it. The building could be seen from the main road, but actually getting there was like a corn maze. The woman on the phone warned it was a bit tricky and tried giving me detailed instruction. Obviously, I wasn't going to bother hoisting my pregnant butt off the couch to grab a pen, so her point was moot. Besides, Siri would know what to do.

But Siri was all "Your destination is to the left" when the only thing to my left was an Applebee's. Eventually I was able to mosey over to the building by driving over a large, grassy median. It was a large strip mall–type building, filled with medical and business offices. Siri kept telling me to turn around until I shouted, "Siri! That's enough! You don't know what you're talking about."

To which she replied, "Calling Tom, the landscaper, now."

"You're done, Siri! You're done!" I turned the car down another street as poor Tom was saying, "Hello? Who's there?" I abruptly ended the call just before hearing, "Are you alright?"

I pulled into a parking spot and noticed there were no less than thirteen doors. It was anyone's guess which one I was supposed to use, but then I remembered the woman on the phone saying, "There will be a potted plant with pink flowers by the door you want to enter," and this helped guide me along. I was greeted by handmade signs that read

"Gestational Diabetes Class" with messy, scribbled arrows. I was about fifteen minutes late and really feeling the heat. I followed the signs until one pointed directly into a classroom. I sighed in frustration when I saw the door was shut, forcing me into an awkward, slow, door-opening situation. Of course, it creaked loudly as it opened and I peeked my head inside. I saw a room full of pregnant women, sitting at tables shaped into a rounded horseshoe. I was greeted by a tall, flamboyant older man with a dark brown beard, wearing a Hawaiian shirt.

"Welcome! You must be Anna," he said, waving his arm and guiding me to an open chair. "I'm Roger Jones, and over there is Nurse Linda Reiner." I smiled, nodding at them both, and took a seat at the rounded curve of the horseshoe. I was surrounded by an array of pregnant women, all of us various shapes, sizes, and ethnicities. Roger handed me the booklet they were all following and directed me to page five.

As I followed along in class, I had to admit parts of it were interesting. My bad attitude slowly evolved into a strong desire to people please. The class suck-up, long dormant, aroused, anxious to demonstrate her smarts and ability to lead.

"Now, what do we do if our blood sugar drops and we begin to feel unwell?" Roger asked the class.

My arm shot up, "Drink apple juice!"

Startled, Roger then nodded in agreement. "Yes, that's certainly a good choice," he looked around the room. "What other healthier alternatives are there?"

I sat back in my chair, smiling, gently caressing my belly. When we went over the nutrition side of things, I took great gratification demonstrating my breadth of health knowledge. My mother had trained me my entire life for that precise moment. I raised my hand, "Mr. Jones?"

"Please, call me Roger."

I cleared my throat. "Excuse me, Roger. What's your take on Ezekiel bread as a healthful carb for breakfast?"

"Fabulous choice," Roger said. "Just be sure to check your sugar after the meal to see how your body handles it." I took a few beats to smile at my cohorts. This class wasn't half bad!

Roger taught us how to clean our hands and properly prick our fingers. He taught us how to use our glucose monitors, check our blood, and what to do if our numbers were too low or too high. Our task was to then document our numbers at specific times for him to review at our next class. I knew this was the perfect opportunity to prove to everyone I didn't have gestational diabetes in the first place.

Naturally, avoiding carbs and sugar seemed like the most obvious way to avoid high blood sugar. Roger basically made carbs out to be a mysterious and powerful food that had to be watched over with excessive vigilance. I'm paraphrasing here, but he'd say, "Don't get weird and hop on a ketogenic diet like you're going on a cruise in a couple weeks." And he'd also say, "If you're in ketosis, eat a piece of toast."

Toast? *Toast? Oh, that's precisely what a bunch of diabetics need, processed white flour!* I couldn't help but sense he didn't know what he was talking about. I specifically told my nurse practitioner they were going to say crazy things, and I was right.

Of course I wouldn't be going on a ketogenic diet, but

you can bet your booty I was avoiding processed carbs and sugar. My mother had taught me well. At home, things went smoothly for a while. I'd eat, wait for the designated amount of time, then check my blood glucose. I was in a safe range nearly every time. In fact, I was so impressed with myself, I daydreamed about one day writing my own nutrition book, providing healthful, wholesome, natural ways of remaining safe and healthy during pregnancy. I'd make it funny too. Gestational diabetes doesn't have to be so serious; let's have a little fun!

Toward the afternoon, I was enjoying a hard-boiled egg with sprinkles of Himalayan salt and fresh cracked pepper, when I noticed a strange sensation. It was a curious feeling, not like anything I'd ever experienced before. But then again, most sensations during pregnancy were something I hadn't experienced before. I poured myself a large glass of fresh spring water, with a squeeze of lemon, and drank heartily. But as I stood at my counter, an unstable avalanche overtook my body. Chills pulsed through me as if I were coming down with the flu. I braced myself against the counter as I became faint, dragging myself to the recliner in my family room, popping the leg rest up and leaning all the way back.

"Rob," I weakly called out, barely louder than a whisper. "Rooooob, heeeeeelp." I listened intently and couldn't hear even a rustle. "Rob!" I shouted, still soft but more throaty. "Rooooob, heeeeelp!"

"Are you talking to me?" Rob asked as he came in the room.

"Who else would I be talking to?" I sat up, annoyed.

"What? What's wrong?"

"Is there any more of that pizza you ate yesterday?" I asked, faintly, my light, dimming.

"Yeah, why?"

"Get some, hurry. Bring it to my lips." Rob walked swiftly in the kitchen and pulled out cold leftover deep-dish meat lover's pizza from the refrigerator.

"Is your blood sugar dropping?" he asked, making his way toward me.

"Less words, more hustle," I said, dazed, lost. He got closer. "Feed me, hurry." Rob put pizza to my lips, and I began eating, slowly and gently at first. As the first bites entered my bloodstream, I picked up the pace, grabbing the pizza on my own and shoveling it into my mouth like a squirrel at a bird feeder. "Another!" I shouted. "Bring me all of it."

"I was sort of wanting it for lunch tomo . . ."

"All of it!" After I aggressively ate it all, I barked for a milkshake. "I don't care where you go, just make it a large!" Rob, now thoroughly confused, but too afraid to question me, hopped in the car to bring me back an assortment of foods not even a '90s nutritionist would recommend. And it helped. After a few pulls on the straw of my chocolate shake, I could feel my body coming back online. At the designated time, I frightfully pricked my finger and checked my blood. How would I ever tell Mr. Jones about this debacle? How I'd been such an arrogant know-it-all who knows nothing at all?

Then Tina whispered in my ear, *Who says you have to tell him anything?*

I won't sugarcoat it; my pregnancies were pure hell. Some women really take to pregnancy. Their bodies are cute and fit with a darling bump. They wear cute maxi dresses. They're the most gorgeous they've ever been, with pregnancy hormones giving them a glow that's almost supernatural. They drink green smoothies and have thirteen professional photo shoots, usually in a field somewhere with a small chalkboard adorned with the month of their pregnancy.

Other women, like me, instantly gain twenty pounds before they even realize they're pregnant. In fact, their newly developed butt meat touching the car door while they run errands is their first clue to pull over and get a pregnancy test. We look haggard, sluggish, and rotate the same three maternity shirts. We wear a full face of makeup, but for some reason, no one can tell. We ingest whatever will go down without puking it up, and we settle for one photo shoot and hate every single photo. We buy at least one of course, because we feel like we have to, but you won't catch us putting that hot mess on Instagram.

Before my pregnancies, I would get migraines during my cycle. I had a certain medication I'd take if it was exceptionally bad, but sometimes over-the-counter medication took the edge off just enough so I could function. But as hormones flooded my body relentlessly in pregnancy, I would get migraines nearly every other week, unable to take medication to ease the pain. I'd spend a third of every month on the couch, a cold, dark cloth over my eyes, as my head thumped violently like a bass drum. Once I had Lucy and was pregnant with Poppy, Rob would often miss work to care for us. Add my gestational diabetes diagnosis, my age, and high-risk status—I had to tell Rob I was terribly sorry, but we were never having sex again.

So, he volunteered to get a vasectomy.

It was all his idea, and he acted like it wasn't a big deal. We were in the kitchen having breakfast when I told him about my friend who wanted her husband to get it done, but her husband refused. "Some men are such selfish babies about it," he said casually, chomping on a banana. "The truth is, it's far less invasive than if a woman gets the procedure done. It's relatively painless and so is recovery. I'll be in and out, no biggie."

But most of his bravado was fueled by the fact his procedure was scheduled a couple months out. It wasn't registering as real. And as the date approached, so did his anxiety. I wanted to be understanding and supportive, but I panicked when he'd say things like, "Remind me again why you hate birth control?"

Terrified he was about to bail, I went into attack mode. "It was my job to have the babies, and now it's your job to make it stop!" But that wasn't helpful, so I changed tactics: "My friend Sharon's husband had it done, and he was playing golf the next day." He knew I didn't have a friend named Sharon, but he readily accepted her husband's success story to have something to cling to.

It was an easy enough outpatient procedure. I stayed home with the girls, and Rob texted me when it was time to pick him up. When I pulled into the curve of the clinic's entrance, Rob was in a wheelchair, looking peaked and frail. I got out and helped him into the passenger seat while he grunted and grimaced.

"Hi, Daddy!" Lucy shouted from the backseat. Rob jumped, covering his hands over his crotch. Lucy was in the backseat, strapped in a car seat, and he was already terrified of her. Just the thought of those loose, careless limbs thrashing about made him nauseated and skittish.

I'm not proud to admit, the drive home tested my patience. He was white-knuckling the "oh crap" handles, drawing sharp breaths at every bump, turn, stop, and go. There were so many "Babe, slow down" and "Watch that bump!" that I almost dropped him off on the nearest curb. He had the drama dial cranked way up, and I was exhausted. I took the girls out of their car seats first and got them inside, then went back for Rob who seemed paralyzed from the neck down. He was still under the effects of pain medication, so it wasn't the pain that paralyzed him; it was the thought of pain to come. He was vulnerable and tender, and even though he couldn't feel pain directly, he felt it deep within his soul.

The girls knew he wasn't feeling well and wanted to be near him, but Rob acted like an abused dog in one of those commercials with photos of helpless animals as Sarah McLachlan sings "Angel." For the rest of the week, he didn't view them as his babies. He saw them as unpredictable Tasmanian devils with flying elbows and knees that were on a mission to destroy whatever was left of his family jewels.

I rolled my eyes so hard, so often, I was developing a slight eyestrain. My father would go to work on his houses with a 104-degree fever. One of his carpenters, Merle, fell off the roof of a home, breaking both his wrists, and he still showed up to the job site the next day. This vasectomy was just a little snip, snap. We've got good drugs. A week off work. I bought him a fresh pack of GMO corn to ice his jewels. Can we put a movie on and move on?

I soon found that when someone is in distress, they aren't comforted when you remind them that you've experienced distress much worse and somehow complained much less. As I reminded him of the state of my vagina after birthing Lucy and how I took it on the chin like a champ, it didn't somehow compel him to rise above his victim mentality as I had hoped.

If pointing out his failings wasn't going to get his mind off his coin purse, maybe food would. I made him chili with cheddar jalapeño cornbread and homemade apple pie with ice cream. I made nachos with fresh guacamole and burgers with pretzel buns. It wasn't the time to worry about heart health; it was all about getting his mind off his man parts. And it seemed to work because over time, he healed, becoming more confident around his children and their uncanny ability to accidentally headbutt his Tom and Harry.

"Do you think we've been too rash?" I asked Rob, casual, as if he hadn't just had his testicles rearranged. We were waiting for test results to see if his vasectomy was a success. It had been a month since his procedure, and I was beginning to second-guess myself. We suffered through three miscarriages and wanted our babies so desperately. And now we're just, *done*? Forever? Did we even think this through?

Yes, my pregnancies were difficult, but truthfully, I could barely remember two weeks of it, let alone nine months. What's the big deal? And yes, I had gestational diabetes, but after the deep-dish pizza debacle, it'd been smooth sailing. And yes, we'd be older parents, but isn't that currently on trend?

"About the vasectomy?" he asked. "Uh, no."

"We might have been *a little* rash."

"Anna, are you serious?" he sat up quickly. "Have you forgotten? We talked through this—we have our two girls; your career is taking off. The sleepless nights? The nursing? There's no way. And your pregnancies! They were a nightmare. No, this was the right choice." He had a point, but I sighed anyway. "Has something happened? What's making you feel this way?"

I was too embarrassed to admit I'd been whipped up by the Christmas spirit. It was the warm coziness of the holidays, and whenever I was out shopping—and maybe it's like when you're thinking about buying a silver Honda Accord, all you see are silver Honda Accords—moms with fresh babies were everywhere I turned. Her teensy little baby wrapped close around her. A fragile angel's head wearing a handsome newsboy cap or pretty little bow. It revved up all my engines. I wanted one! I missed one! *I needed one.* I consistently held a vision of a newborn pairing delightfully each morning with my cup of coffee. The two of us cozy, the baby dozing while I read a good book.

But then I wondered, *Maybe I don't want an actual baby, I just wanted baby ambiance.* Like a lit candle while praying, or Ella Fitzgerald while hosting a dinner party. Maybe I just wanted a sweet newborn during my morning quiet time with God, with a high-end French press and a really good pen.

"It's nothing," I assured him. "Really, you're right. I don't know what I was thinking." I got up to make an afternoon chai tea, and Rob had moved on so quickly, he was in the beginning stages of a nap.

I think God has us easily forget how difficult the first couple years are with a child so that we'll foolishly keep doing it again and again. But we were getting older. Our lives were changing. I was sad the newborn season of my life was over but simultaneously knew it was time.

Within the hour, we got an alert that Rob's test results were in. We were officially done having babies.

"Now," Roger continued, working the room in wide loops, "if you choose to have another pregnancy, your chance of getting gestational diabetes again goes up by about 60 percent, but that's not always the case . . ." he continued on, but my mind began to wander. I could feel Poppy kick, and I touched the area with my hand, softly rubbing what I assumed to be her teeny heel. I knew instinctively she was my last baby, so I tried to treasure that feeling of having her inside my womb. To take a mental picture so I wouldn't forget.

The class had about ten minutes left, and I had to pee with the volume and velocity of a fire hose. I pardoned myself and made my way into the restroom.

After I was done, I washed my hands and gazed at my reflection. My face was rounder, softer. My cheekbones undefined. I swore I had on makeup, but my face looked light, fresh, and clean. I must say, I looked beautiful. I was carrying a child. And I knew I must do everything I could to protect her. I had tumbled down pride mountain real hard, but now I was calm. Humbled. I had the class booklet, I took important notes, time to get on with it.

I grabbed my purse and made my way down the hallway, stopping short before going back into class. "Tell us one thing you've learned that you plan to put into action," I heard Roger say.

I kept walking, right past the class, through the parking lot, back to my car. The class was almost over anyway; it was probably fine. Besides, if Tina taught me anything—*they're not the boss of me.*

I'm the boss.

CHAPTER 10
Come On Over

Where's Christian?" My brother was noticeably absent from the pew. Mom and Dad were there, but where was he? Most Sundays, our family gets together for church, and we usually have lunch together afterward. Christian's absence wouldn't normally cause alarm, but he invited us over for lunch, and I was already starving.

"He's not coming," my mom whispered. Worship had

just begun, so we were doing that loud whisper thing people do in church or at their great-aunt's funeral. "He called this morning and said he wanted to let CJ sleep in and get some rest." That was an odd thing to say. CJ was four, not ninety-four.

"So, in other words, he didn't get the sauce on in time," I whispered back.

"Exactly."

My brother is a burly master electrician, but his dream has always been to sell our family's Sicilian tomato sauce. Each of us have our own way of making the sauce. Our Sicilian grandmother used mostly tomato paste, as do my aunts, and my mom uses whatever's in the cupboard. I use a combination of sauce, purée, and whole tomatoes. The way we season varies, too, but what those ingredients are remains the same. Christian uses giant handfuls of our dried herbs and seasonings, where I'm a bit more modest. My sister uses a half cup of sugar. Mom drops in entire cloves of garlic; I mince a bulb and go nuts. But in the end, it's all generally the same and equally delicious.

This was his first time hosting our family, and it meant a lot to him. When we arrived, the first thing I noticed was the sweat dripping down my brother's forehead. The house was pristine, but he was a hot mess. It's the kind of sweat that happens to a man when he's on the side of the road changing a tire during the dog days of summer. Anyone who's hosted even a simple coffee date knows the kind of stress a newbie would be under. The sauce was bubbling away on the stove, burning a little, and on his kitchen table he put out slices of watermelon, precut and still covered in plastic wrap, with a barcode. Mom was in the kitchen with Christian, and he had a distant, lost look in his eye. He'd scuttle about quickly, then disappear for ten minutes to God knows where, only to emerge as if he had made a wrong turn somewhere.

My mom has always said you never leave a hungry crowd waiting. I think it's because, due to her own experience, the crowd will turn on you. Anticipating this, and wanting to help my brother succeed in his endeavor to treat us, mom had brought just a few things to hold us over until the meal was ready. From her little thermal bag, she pulled out vegetables, dip, and olives for a veggie tray, crackers, a baguette, and various cheeses. I don't know what it is about church, but once I sense the pastor has about thirty minutes left, I get wild with hunger. I call them the Church Hangries, because that's precisely what it is. I'm talking the kind of starvation that makes you snap at your husband carrying on with *way too much* small talk with the pastor. Oddly, at 11:00 a.m. during Monday through Saturday, none of that possessive hunger ever happens to me. In fact, if I'm busy, I can make it to early afternoon before I start thinking about eating. But at church, something weird triggers me, and I'm nearly faint. So, when Mom started pulling out veggies, I started biting into celery, reaching around her for crackers, and crawling through her legs to get to the soft cheese. "When are you slicing up that baguette?" I asked, rummaging in her bag.

"I, um, I was the one, um, hosting, Mom," Christian interrupted. "This is all my treat. You didn't need to bring anything."

145

"Oh!" she said, peeling a carrot. "Well, you're doing so much, I thought I'd help the host with a little vegetable tray."

Of course, this back-and-forth was nothing more than verbal jujitsu masquerading as pleasantries. Christian felt annoyed and threatened Mom had moved into his territory, and Mom knew Christian would be underprepared to feed a church crowd, so starved they'd go in the backyard and shoot a squirrel if someone didn't feed them quick.

This wasn't her first rodeo. My mom knows how to put on a family event; it's etched in her muscle memory. It's not like a wine party, where people assume the evening will go slow and food trickles through while everyone socializes. At family events, people are there to eat. We talk to each other all the time; we don't need to get together to keep talking forever. Family get-togethers have gone wrong so many times, she knows how to make it right. She knows, for instance, you can't tell people to come at five o'clock and not have the roast done until seven. My sister pulled that crap on us more than a decade ago, and not a single one of us have let it go. Also, you want to put some food out to take the edge off, but not so much they just pick at the main course. Keep silverware and napkins easily accessible or, instead of eating, everyone will roam around opening drawers. And good grief, give the kids their own table, or they'll take all the good seats and ruin the whole thing.

Christian, still learning, failed to hit these key success points. And instead of accepting Mom's help, continued to resist.

"I don't want people to get stuffed on all this and not

want my spaghetti," he protested, taking a towel to his face, neck, and chest.

"Don't be silly!" I said from the family room. I was deep into the Church Hangries and starting to unravel. It appeared the sauce still had an hour left to simmer, and I had anxiety up to my eyeballs—if the woman wants to put out some crackers and black olives, get out of her way and let her do what she does best. "No one will get stuffed, Christian, I promise."

"Yes, just relax and focus on getting the water going for the pasta," Mom said, slicing the carrots into sticks. "I won't put out too much, don't worry."

He busied himself putting on the water, occasionally stirring the sauce. It was sweet how much it all meant to him. He really wanted to treat us and make sure we had a wonderful time. He ran over and poured me a glass of red wine. "Oh, fanc*aaaay*," I said, taking a sip.

"That's a forty-dollar bottle," he said, gesturing to me. "You can tell the difference, can't you?"

"Mm-hmm," I assured him. "Tastes so good." But the truth was, that could have been a jug of Carlo Rossi and I'd be none the wiser. I love the idea of being a wine connoisseur, but I don't have the stamina or the budget. Even so, there was this one time when I was at my friend's house and really surprised myself. Her dad loved wine, often collecting it, going to various wine tastings, even in Italy, taking it all very seriously. He poured me a glass, showed me how to swish it around, then instructed me to tip the glass toward my nose, sniff deeply for smell, before letting the wine hit my tongue for taste. Always the diligent student, I did as I was told.

"Now," he said, watching me intently, "tell me what you taste."

I was nervous because all I could really taste was wine. But I thought real hard and said, "Well, I think I taste strawberries."

"No, there are no strawberries in here," he said matter-of-factly, looking at the back of the bottle. I shrugged and then took a real sip, the kind where I'm ready to cut loose and see what's up with the jalapeño poppers. "Oh wait," he said, surprised. "Well, I'll be. There are strawberries in here."

I must say, I wasn't surprised. I don't want to brag, but I pretty much nail everything I try the first time. I guess it's a crazy bout of beginner's luck, and I have to strike while the iron's hot before it fizzles. My bloated self-confidence, thanks to being the baby in the family, mixed with being a newbie and having nothing to lose gets me out of my own way to simply get the job done.

When I was in high school, my friend Brett signed us up as a team for a two-on-two basketball tournament. It was for fun, but by the looks of everyone who signed up, it was taken very seriously. Mind you, I'd never played basketball a day in my life. My friend was no ace, but he at least knew where you stood for a free throw. But I agreed because, who cares? Hand to God, every time my hand touched the ball, it was nothing but net. You should have seen me hit that dagger three. *Clutch.* We made it all the way to the semifinals. My only complaint was my friend passed the ball way too hard. When that thing slaps, it stings.

When Rob and I were dating, he took me to a putt-putt course in Roseville, California. Rob and I have always been deadly competitive against each other, even in the early days when we should have been more focused on becoming potential life partners. Still, I was fully prepared to rip out his ego and humiliate him. The last time I held a putter was when I was eight years old, but no problem. I left that place with a near perfect score. On the last hole, I hit the windmill, causing my ball to fly in the air, hit a fake tree, ricochet four times, then slowly crawl right into the hole. A young employee was standing nearby and saw the whole thing. "Holy crap, dude! I've never seen anything like that!" His expression read like he just had a UFO hovering over him. Thrilled and a little scared, he continued, "Like, wow. I can't even . . . I'm speechless! Unbelievable, dude. Wow."

Rob, now deeply annoyed, barked, "Alright man, we get it, okay? Calm down." He was real pissy after his humiliating loss, and I was tickled pink. Still to this day, Rob gets annoyed at the high praise I receive. Just two weeks ago, while fishing for the first time, I cast the rod with ease, shocking my brother-in-law, and caught a huge bass two minutes later. "Fish on!" I screamed from the beach, a term I learned by watching every season of the reality series *Alaska: The Last Frontier.*

"Are you sure you've never done this before?" my brother-in-law asked.

"John, please don't," Rob moaned from a nearby folding chair.

Of course, the list goes on and on. The only trouble is,

after my first slam dunk, things tend to go downhill after my rational mind finally catches up and realizes I literally have no idea what I'm doing. Then I become normal, having to learn to be great the hard way, through practice and perseverance. Who has the time?

Anyway, after Christian poured me the wine, Mom then moved in with a plate of various cheeses, including an aged cherry cheese that was really something. "Now don't eat too much and get stuffed," she said in a hushed tone to me and my dad, already sitting at the table. "Christian is really excited about his spaghetti, so don't ruin your appetite." Then she grabbed the wrapped watermelon slices Christian set out and hid them behind a bowl.

"Why is everyone worrying?" I said. "Don't worry!" I had already crunched on a celery stick and downed two crackers. Rob, who had been sitting in the living room perusing his phone, walked in.

"Are we eating or what?" he asked, throwing his weight around. "Oh, what's that? The cheese looks good."

"We're just eating a little bit," I whispered, trying to get him to calm down and play it cool.

"Yeah, Rob, nice and slow. Christian doesn't want us to get full on these appetizers," Mom said sternly, trying to speak without moving her lips.

"Okay, geez," he said, piling crackers, bread, and cheese onto a plate. "I'll have room to eat. Everyone relax."

But once I started cracking on the cherry cheese, I couldn't contain myself. Honestly, I should have known. There has never been one time when I haven't fully stuffed myself on the free bread they give you at restaurants. I don't just take a modest slice to take the edge off; I go all in, elbowing my husband and kids for the butter, then nodding sheepishly at the server when he asks if we'd like more. And so, naturally, when my actual meal arrives, I approach it with cautious interest, like a huge slice of pie after Thanksgiving dinner. "Wow, I mean, wow, this cheese!" I looked around, making eye contact with everyone, an expression of pure delight.

"Isn't it good?" Mom said. "It's raw too."

"This cherry? I mean, incredible!"

My brother turned around from the stove, sweat dripping like condensation off a jug of lemonade. "Pasta's almost done, don't go too crazy on the starters," he said. "I want you nice and hungry when you try my version of the Marino sauce." You could tell he was really getting anxious, watching all his hard work go right down the tubes with Mom's fancy cheese. I'm not sure what he did after that. I was too busy eating vegetables, dipping them heartily, and really enjoying the assortment of crackers.

"I mean, why are Wheat Thins so good?" I asked no one in particular. Christian went missing again, and Mom got the pasta off the stove and into a colander. What happened next scared me. I swear, I didn't mean for it to happen. Surely a veggie tray and some fancy cheese couldn't take me down; I'm a robust woman. But it did. I sat for a long while in denial, but eventually I had to face it.

"Mom, oh no, oh no. I've got bad news," I said in a hushed tone, grabbing her shoulder and pulling her toward me.

"What? What is it?" she whispered.

"I'm stuffed."

"*What?*" she shouted, surprising even herself, before looking around to see if Christian was around. She grabbed my arm and dragged me into the family room.

"What do you mean, you're stuffed?"

"I, I, I'm just stuffed. *To the gills*. What do I do?" I pleaded.

"How could you let yourself get stuffed like this?" she snapped.

"You think I wanted to get stuffed?" I cried. "You think I wanted this?"

"Well, you clearly didn't try to prevent it."

"It was the cheese!" I cried. "It's incredible!"

"Don't you go blaming the cheese. This is on you." She looked over her shoulder to make sure Christian wasn't in earshot.

"What are you guys whispering about over there," Rob asked from across the room.

"Shut up, Rob!" we both yelled in unison.

"Geez," Rob mumbled before scrolling through his phone.

"Sorry, babe, but can't you see we're in the middle of a crisis?" I threw at him, then turned back to my mom. "It was an accident, Mom. Help me."

"Oh, Anna," she said, clearly pained. "He specifically asked us to not get stuffed. And I assured him we wouldn't get stuffed. You looked him dead in the eyes and told him you wouldn't get stuffed. And here you are. Stuffed!"

"I know!" I wailed, but as quietly as I could.

"Your brother worked so hard for this."

I moaned. "What do I do?"

"You march over to him and give him an apology, that's what you do," she said, attempting to return to the kitchen.

I grabbed her arm again, "Are you insane? I'm not admitting I got stuffed. I'll try and eat as much spaghetti as I can. He'll never know."

"Let's pray he doesn't." Disappointed, she headed back into the kitchen for damage control.

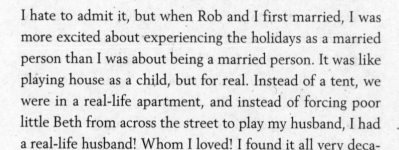

I hate to admit it, but when Rob and I first married, I was more excited about experiencing the holidays as a married person than I was about being a married person. It was like playing house as a child, but for real. Instead of a tent, we were in a real-life apartment, and instead of forcing poor little Beth from across the street to play my husband, I had a real-life husband! Whom I loved! I found it all very decadent and exciting.

When I was single, my mom or my sister were the ones hosting the holidays. They created the holiday magic, and I was just told when to show up. But now that I was grown, it was my time to shine in my own home. And Easter was coming! I bought a *Cook's Illustrated*, and I was gonna make a ham. And maybe even scalloped potatoes if the recipe didn't seem too hard.

But my sister wasn't having it. She invited us to her house so aggressively, I felt like I had to come. If she'd been thinking clearly, she'd know adding two extra people to her table was the last thing she needed. But this is the thing about my sister; she gets really excited about hosting large gatherings, especially on the holidays. She licks her pen and starts planning the food, all worked up at the possibilities. She's a brilliant cook, and even I have to admit, the planning-the-food part is the best part. But what she forgot, especially when her children were young, was that she's a mother of eight, exhausted to the point of collapse, and liked *the thought* of throwing huge parties far more than actually throwing them.

She'd go from welcoming us to resenting us before I could take my coat off. Honestly, I get it. What I find most egregious about hosting is the cleaning beforehand. And my family helps me the best they can, but I become the Gordon Ramsay from *Hell's Kitchen* of housecleaning. I can't be satisfied, and nothing they do is good enough. It's the only time I notice, with disgust, dust on my baseboards. My guests will be arriving soon, yet I'll be on my hands and knees with a wet rag tracing the walls, as a growing resentment toward my husband, who has chosen to enjoy his life by not caring, seeps from my pores.

Rob will come into the room and take pity on me. "Babe, this isn't necessary; no one's looking at the baseboards."

"Just because *you* don't notice filthy baseboards doesn't mean *I* don't notice filthy baseboards," I bark. Realizing the mistake he made, Rob slowly exits the room backward before I add, "Instead of encouraging me *to not* do something, why don't you pick up a rag and do something!"

Like clockwork, about an hour before guests arrive, I turn on my family. In fact, it's so predictable, our English bulldog, Bruno, has learned a series of certain behaviors from me equals people coming into his home—inspiring him to run to the door and bark. Just as he whimpers when I put on real-people clothes because it means I'm leaving, he runs to the door when I'm completely disheveled, yelling at my family to pick up their crap.

The day before I host a gathering, I'm quite joyful. The promise of charitable hospitality, the warmth of family, friends, and cherished memories give me pep and energy. But after hours of backbreaking work, my mood sours.

"Why is this teddy bear on the floor? I told you all to pick this up and put it in your room!" I yell. Then I march across the room. "Whose cup is this? I'm serious, who left this cup here? Put it in the dishwasher!" Then I stomp across the other direction, making an X on the carpet, "I swear I'm the only one who does *anything* around here." Then I turn with angry eyes, "Rob, go take the trash out and while you're out there, rake the leaves! The whole neighborhood thinks we're the lazy, trash house!" And just like that, Bruno receives all he needs to know, and off he goes to the door to bark aggressively at an empty driveway. "Bruno, shut up! They won't be here for another hour!"

Then I just stand there, locked in fear. They'll arrive any minute, and I'm not even close to ready. My Roomba bumps repetitively into my ankle.

I'm not sure if Jenny turns on her family as I do, but I do know she turns on her guests. When I'm invited to a family gathering, it's customary to ask, "What should I bring?" and she always says, "Nothing, just your happy self!" Of course, it's a trap. When you ask her that question, she's still relishing her hosting high that hasn't yet plummeted back to reality. But if you walk through that door without so much as some Hawaiian sweet rolls, God help you.

Typically, when you enter her home, you say "Helloooooo," as you enter, then as you make your way into the kitchen, you'll see her standing there with a fake smile. "Hey," she says, "did you bring any rolls?" She's completely exhausted by the time you arrive and probably has a headache, wishing she just followed her gut and called the whole thing off.

One of the worst mistakes you can make is to actually enjoy yourself. This will only reinforce the injustice she's endured. Not only has she been deep cleaning for two days, grocery shopping, prepping and cooking, breaking up fights between her kids, and barking at her husband to give the walls a fresh coat of paint, the last thing she wants to see is you having a great time while she's chained to the stove, whisking the gravy.

On this particular Easter, I could tell the moment I walked in, she was stressed. Had I been a neighbor or friend, I'm sure she would've faked her enthusiasm upon my entrance, but since I'm her sister, she hid nothing. To be honest, *I wish she would have hid a little something.*

"Helloooooooo," I said, entering her home empty-handed, per her request. Rob and I didn't have the girls yet, so it was just us.

"Hey," she said, bent over in the oven, checking the ham. Then she popped up. "You didn't bring anything?"

"Well, I asked, and you said not to."

"I could have used some rolls."

"Well, I can go get . . ."

"No, it's fine," she said, cutting me off. I noticed she had a limp. Two of her youngest children were hanging off her body like monkeys.

As the rest of the family trickled in, we carried on with our typical banter. Some of us with wine or a beer, eating our plate of Easter fare. "No beans?" I asked, while putting scalloped potatoes on my plate. My intent behind the question was benign, but I might as well have thrown a glass of wine in her face.

"My family hates beans," she said flatly.

"I could have brought some . . ." I trailed off as she started digging through her cupboard where the Advil was kept.

After my second glass of wine, I started really feeling myself, cracking jokes at the kitchen table. To add insult to injury, most of our family have an incredibly loud laugh, and the louder the laughter, the louder she started throwing dishes in the dishwasher.

"Wow, just wow," she mumbled to herself, crashing dishes in. I was having too much fun to notice she had started cleaning up, but once the clanking hit a crescendo, it couldn't be ignored.

"Jenny, can we help?"

"Nope, all done," she said, slapping the door closed.

Over the years, I'd start to take on more hosting responsibilities, but because her family is so large, it always made sense for her to host more often. "Come on over!" she'd say on the phone, full of pep and American cheer. We're grilling for the Fourth and have tons of food. Just bring your happy self!" But of course, I knew better.

I brought the beans.

As I walked in with my Old Navy American flag shirt and my casserole dish, I said, "Helloooooooo," where I met my sister, tanned like she was a teenage lifeguard, sort of happy to see me, but mostly wanting a nap.

"Did you bring any hot dog buns?" she asked. But, of course, I hadn't.

"No, but I can go . . ."

"No, it's fine," she said behind her shoulder, rooting through her purse. "Where's my Advil?"

Christian laid my pasta plate before me, and I selected a couple choice meatballs from the center bowl. While it looked delicious and I felt so proud of him, I was stuffed with cheese up to my clavicle. If he had placed a piece of pumpkin pie before me, I'm sure I could have somehow found the strength to persevere, but a meatball? Everyone else had their plates piled high, my girls eating heartily with their cousin Christian Jr. at the kid's table. I felt relieved—everyone else was eating well, the perfect cover to hide behind. I sat back and sipped my wine. I took a few bites here and there, moving the noodles around just so. Then Christian piped up, "Did you ever see the jar labels I made for our family sauce?" About a year ago, he took bottling our family recipe and selling it *very seriously*, but then the great downer of reality struck when questions were asked like, "Is this kitchen up to code?" and "What's the plan to introduce this to the marketplace?"

He pulled out his phone, thumbed through a few photos, then landed on the one. The entire label was just a black-and-white photo of our grandma, Sebastiana, whom everyone lovingly called Nettie. She was young and looked like a movie star. I remember her as a round, Sicilian grandma with short gray hair. I don't have many memories of her, but I do have one I think about often. I spent the entire day with her, and she had a pot of sauce on the stove. She made her sauce at least once a week, and it was always available on holidays, too, per my grandpa's request.

I sat in her kitchen while she stirred, tasted, added more salt, sipped from a wooden spoon, then stirred again. I could hear a football game on in the other room, my grandpa sleeping in his recliner. She always kept a pack of Trident gum in the drawer next to the stove.

"Grandma?" I asked.

"Hmm?"

"Can I have some gum?"

"Sure, honey," she said, dipping her wooden spoon into the pot. "But first, grandma wants you to try her sauce."

After she blew to cool it down, she put the spoon to my lips for a sip. It tasted the way it's always tasted. Sweet, rich, and flavorful. The secret has always been the anise seed she crushed in her soft, aging hand before sprinkling it in. The same anise seed crushed in my brother's thick, calloused hand today.

"It's perfect, Grandma," I said, pulling out a piece of gum.

"Of course it is."

She wiped her hands on a kitchen towel. "Let's go find

some extra chairs for Jenny and Christian." My family would be arriving soon to join us for dinner before taking me home. I grabbed her hand and followed her to the dining room. I was a little hungry, but you couldn't rush the sauce. It bubbled and popped on the stove, as it always has, for generations. It had about one more hour to simmer, my family set to arrive shortly after.

Then, and only then, would it be time to eat.

CHAPTER 11
Impressive

E veryone's entitled to an off day, except my hairstylist.
I'll concede that hairstylists are people, too, I guess,
but because they hold great power, they must acknowledge
its great responsibility. It's not my fault she chose a career
that makes me needy, emotional, and codependent.

In the same vein, I believe everyone's entitled to change
careers and pursue their dream. Except my hairstylist. She

made her hairstyling bed, seduced me with her talent, and should lie in it for as long as I needed her services. But, no. Shortly after I delivered my baby Poppy, Gina betrayed me.

Her timing couldn't have been worse. I was experiencing postnatal hair loss to such an extreme, my hairline receded like I was Jack Nicholson letting the back grow long. Once Poppy started eating soft foods, it grew back ever so slowly, little curlies bordering my forehead. It was time to reclaim my dignity—I picked up the phone and called Gina.

"I'm sorry, Gina no longer works at this salon," said the young woman at the front desk. My blood ran cold. "Would you like to schedule an appointment with one of our other . . ." I hung up before she could finish.

Five years prior, I found Gina by doing a search through various upscale salons located downtown. That may seem uppity, but I needed to find a stylist experienced with curly hair, and in my experience, hairstylists were liars. Well, okay, that's not entirely true. But if you're a curly haired woman on the hunt for someone who actually knows what they're doing, you'll find you have to wade through a sea of stylists who love the *idea* of cutting and styling curly hair far more than they actually know *how* to cut and style curly hair. I suppose if I'm being honest with myself, I know the feeling.

For instance, I love the *idea* of scrapbooking. My children's entire lives are stored in my iPhone, and it makes me feel vulnerable and irresponsible. Every time I upgrade to a new phone, I start to sweat, thinking I might accidentally lose their entire childhood while transferring data. When I was young, my mom was oblivious to how good she had it.

Sure, she didn't have the luxury of having her picture taken, instantly review it horrified, then demand the person behind the camera try again thirty-six more times. But I hope Mom experienced a great sense of freedom when she just "clicked" and that was it. The end result was out of her hands. No filters, no lighting adjustments, no cropping, what's done was done, and life could go on. Once the film was spent, she dropped it off at Walgreens, praying for at least one decent shot that could go in a frame. The anticipation may be intense, but at least she was motivated to have actual photographs you can touch and store for safekeeping. The limited space on film gave her boundaries and proper cues. I have no less than 39,378 photos of my children just sitting in my phone, and the sheer number has paralyzed me. I guess there are apps where I can print them all in a book, but do I really want some paperback book of pictures? I can store them in a cloud of some sort, but do I really want to pay a picture-hoarding fee? Okay, fair enough, I can digitally upload them to a service and have them printed, but can I afford 39,378 glossy prints, or do I have to sift and choose which ones are worthy? I'm too exhausted to even keep talking about this.

So yes, scrapbooking has its appeal. But when I got home with the $200 worth of craft supplies sprawled before me, I realized I talked a big game, with no real clue about what I'd gotten myself into. *What am I supposed to do with this mess?* I wondered.

And this is the same countenance I've seen on the faces of countless stylists as I sit before them. Sure, on the phone, they talked that big curly game, but once I book the appointment and sit in their chairs, I get the same disenchanted look, every time. *What am I supposed to do with this mess?*

The look appears concerned and focused, as if they're trying to figure out what a 20 percent tip would be after a few dirty martinis. And I get it, curly hair is rebellious and unpredictable. They don't know how it'll react once they start cutting. The top layer is usually curlier with more spring, while the hair underneath is longer with less curl. Cut it too short and I'll look like George Washington with a Billy Ray Cyrus mullet in the back. I'm under no illusion about the complexity of the task at hand. I then complicate things by requesting a little color, perhaps some highlights to give my hair dimension and interest. With straight hair, this is pretty straightforward, but with curly hair, who knows what you're gonna get. After an intense deliberation, I can see both fear and resolve in their eyes before they gather their courage and bravely step forward.

As the recipient of this inexperienced courage, it ain't great. This is my hair we're talking about, not a deliberation about how we'll go about trimming some hedges. I recall one stylist who had me brush out my own hair. "I don't want to hurt you," she said, frightened. In her defense, I wash my hair weekly and toward the end it starts to get matted like a neglected Shih Tzu's butt. In *my* defense, there was no reason to brush my hair out in the first place. Unless, of course, she was trying to make my hair *as straight as possible*—a clear tell she had no idea what to do with that mess. The last straw was when a stylist, in a popular strip mall salon, botched my layers. She then dyed it the color of soot and gave me thin, white highlights all over. To complete the look, I just needed to pluck my eyebrows into long, thin, arching lines and trace them with a fine-point pen. Once she started blow-drying it without a diffuser, I had to call it quits. I didn't want to hurt her feelings, so I said I was running late to a meeting and would prefer it air-dry. As I turned to leave, she said, "Hey, when it dries, can you text me a picture so I can see how it turned out? I've never done curly hair like that before."

Of course, that much was obvious, but I felt compelled to set the record straight. "Weird, because when I called, the front desk said you loved doing all sorts of curly hair." I then gave her *Golden Girls'* Dorothy Zbornak eyes as she let her smile fall.

Needless to say, I'd been burned so many times, I thought I might live my entire life without ever experiencing a hair-stylist I truly loved.

And then I met Gina.

I narrowed my search to upscale salons in the hopes that the more I paid, the more they knew what they were doing. There was a nice-looking salon downtown, on the edge of the Old Market. I perused the bios of their stylists, and Gina stuck out immediately. She was gorgeous, a Latina Dua Lipa with cool Kat Von D vibes. I wanted to be her, hate her, and be best friends, all at the same time. Her profile on the salon's website said she specialized in curly hair, so I wasted no time making the appointment.

I hate to admit it, but Gina could have suggested we shave my head bald and I would've gone for it. Walking into the salon made me feel like Mama June stumbling into the

Met Gala—I felt pathetic in her presence. But what really sealed the deal was how she beautifully cut and colored my hair with such confidence and ease. Any woman will tell you, a talented hairstylist is more precious than silver. But when you have curly hair, they're so precious, you'd consider kidnapping them and locking them away in your basement if they ever made a career change.

That's why, when I rang up Gina's salon as my curl regrowth roared back with an early-2000s Justin Timberlake vengeance, I was tempted to slip into despair and hunt down her home address. I clung to hope, however, that she may have simply moved to another salon. Gina and I were Facebook friends, so I messaged her directly: "Hey you! I just called to make an appointment, but they said you aren't there anymore. What salon are you at now?"

After an excruciating twenty-four hours, she finally responded: "Hey, babe, so sorry, but I'm not a stylist anymore. I've decided to pursue a dream of mine and started my own business. Give Tracy a try, though—she's great. I know you'll love her."

The gall of that arrogant, self-absorbed woman. So, what, she was going to pursue her dream without running it by me first? Like, what am I supposed to do now, go to Tracy? Isn't that the stylist who has bleach-blond pigtails and wears clothes suited for a vampire's funeral? I'm putting my foot down. No!

I was so forlorn, I didn't wash my hair for days on end. I just didn't have it in me to look for another stylist, so I let my hair grow long until I appeared to be in a religious cult where women are forbidden to cut their hair. I realized it was time to wake from my grief when I filmed a marketing video for my dad's business. It's hard to explain what I looked like, but imagine if Michelle Duggar tried to grow her hair out to look like '90s Alanis Morissette. Once I saw it, I knew I owed it to myself to find a new stylist.

This time I got straight to the point and googled, "Best curly-hair stylist in Omaha," and to my relief, a woman popped up named Melanie. She was a curly-hair specialist (fancy!) and was mentioned in a local news article. I called to set an appointment and was told her next available was in four months. Apparently curly-hair specialists are so in demand, I'd be able to fling from trees like Rapunzel by the time it's my turn.

When Gina styled my hair, we talked each other's ears off, sharing every tawdry detail of our lives. I told her things I wouldn't have confessed to Dr. Ruth, and she told me things that could've put her in jail. But that's the great mystery of the stylist's chair—it summons secrets, deeply personal anecdotes, and hot gossip like it's a Truth or Dare slumber party. As Melanie walked up to the waiting area to collect me, however, her vibes informed me that we wouldn't have the same rapport. This was business, not TMI, so keep the bikini wax story to yourself.

Melanie was cute, friendly, and stylish, but it only took a few minutes to realize she didn't have the temperament for small talk and only suffered through it as part of the job. I recognized this part of her temperament because I saw bits of myself in her demeanor. I'm always friendly, but I'm only chatty when I'm vulnerable and needy, interacting with someone who is helping me in some way. Stylists, consultants, photographers, agents, gynecologists—you get the idea. Still, I wondered how an introvert who just wants to be left alone could survive working a job that's known for its salacious, deeply personal small talk more than its actual hairstyling?

As she sat me down and asked a few basic questions about my hair, I smelled wafts of indifference. Maybe it's because I'm the baby of the family, or maybe it's the whole "hard-to-get" phenomenon, but I was miffed and determined to do something about it. It's not that she was unfriendly or didn't like me; she just didn't care either way. Unfortunately, her aloofness triggered a part of me, whom I'll call Tammy, who was up for the challenge, determined to impress her. Melanie would adore me by the time the last curl dried, so help me God.

I felt I made some headway when she laid my hair down to examine it. "I understand I look a little bit like Michelle Duggar with an Alanis Morissette obsession," I joked. That made her laugh. This was her first mistake, because it encouraged me to keep going at a pace that isn't normal in a typical human interaction. I shared how Gina left the business and how difficult it has been to find another stylist who's truly good at cutting curly hair. At that comment, I felt Tammy gurgling inside me, trying to brag, not about me, but about Gina. Weird flex, but I guess Tammy figured if Gina was my hairstylist, then I, too, must be gorgeous, cool, and fashionable by proxy? Who knows?

The practical side of me, whom I'll call Carol, tried to protect me from humiliating myself and intervened. "Now, Tammy," she said, "Melanie doesn't want to hear about how gorgeous and cool Gina is, okay? That's weird. Just calm down and let her do her job." But Tammy was a bull in a china shop and couldn't be contained. She not only went on and on about Gina, she took it a step further, taking out my phone and showing her Gina's Instagram. Carol died a million deaths.

"Isn't she so fashionable and gorgeous? Like, she should be a famous stylist in LA, not running some business in Omaha," I said, like a buffoon. I cringed; Carol cringed. Someone put us out of our misery.

"Cool," Melanie said, snipping at my hair. She was polite enough, but that had to put her off, how could it not? The topic alone created an awkward comparison. I noticed a redness spreading across my chest in the mirror, but I assured myself there was still time to recover my dignity. I took a deep breath and tried to relax.

Melanie used a technique I hadn't seen before, cutting at my hair randomly, snipping away like Edward Scissorhands. But my hair began to take a perfect shape. It bounced and fell just right, stylish and beautiful, in a way Gina was never able to do. Unfortunately, Melanie's skills only served to turbocharge my obsession with dismantling her indifference. "Tammy, this is too desperate!" Carol pleaded, but Tammy wanted positive affirmation, no matter the cost. And at that, I simply started bragging.

I bragged about losing twenty pounds, "Bottom line, most of us simply eat too much, too often." I bragged about my family's Sicilian tomato sauce, "Everyone who has tried it says it's the best they've ever had, I'll bring you a sample at my next appointment." I bragged about my triceps, "I'm as surprised as anybody that simply picking up my children has created such definition." I bragged about my kids, "My friend thinks I should get Poppy into child modeling, but I want her to have a normal childhood, you know?" Carol and I were dejected and humiliated. Tammy just kept going and going, with no end in sight. After a brief pause to sip my complimentary coffee, I continued, unprovoked, "So, I'm a writer." Melanie met eyes with me in the mirror before I added, "I would ask what you do, but I guess it's obvious." Then I let out this weird laugh I didn't even recognize. Tammy was fishing, of course, hoping to reel in follow-up questions so she could brag about my book deal.

"Oh, that's cool," she said, snipping and smiling kindly. A young woman from the front desk approached her and asked her a question quietly. "That's fine, just reschedule it," Melanie told her, then went back to snipping my hair.

Hmmm, dead end. I cleared my throat.

"Yeah, I um, got a book deal, and I'm writing my first book now."

"Oh?" she said. "What do you write? Fiction? Nonfiction?"

"I'm a humor writer," I said. "I mostly write personal essays."

"Cool." Snip, snip, snip. I think I could have been Oprah and it wouldn't have made a difference. The woman was the Fort Knox of not giving a crap. If I had even one shred of dignity left, I would've left the poor girl alone to cut in introverted peace. All I wanted to do was recede, sit quietly, and look at my phone.

But not Tammy. She wasn't getting results and doubled down. Sensing Carol and I resisting, she casually suggested we bring up my upcoming appearance on a TV show on a major network. Carol wasn't having it. "Absolutely not, Tammy. Have you no shame?"

"Ugh, you guys are so lame," Tammy said. "Just trust me. I'll bait her with something benign so we can bring it up without it being weird. It's fine, I got this."

"So," I said, squiggling in my chair, "ever been on TV?" *Oh, come on!*

"Can't say I have," Melanie said. "You?"

"Funny you should ask—I've just been cast for a TV show airing next fall." Carol collapsed. "Yeah, it's crazy," Tammy continued. "A casting agent just called me up out of the blue. They want me to share one of my funniest stories with celebrity hosts." I narrowed my eyes, hoping Melanie would ask follow-up questions for more details.

"That's cool! Hey, I'll be right back. I need to go mix up your color."

This was a disaster. I gave her everything I got, and she simply did not care. A TV show? Hello? This woman would never be impressed. As I waited, my body flooded with various, conflicting emotions. Carol and I begged Tammy to please just stop. *Give us a sliver of self-respect, please.* We were so far past embarrassing, we were now flirting with "the curly haired girl with problems." I couldn't bear to look myself in the face, but I had to admit my hair was looking really good. Melanie returned and methodically added a foilyage highlight effect on my hair. It took all my strength to be quiet. Tammy was a fighter, and she wasn't going down easy. Suppressing her felt like holding my breath underwater, painful and unsustainable. I couldn't take it anymore. "My manuscript is due in June!" I blurted out. Melanie jumped.

"Really? So soon?" You had to give her credit for how she balanced a polite rapport without actively encouraging me for more information. Tammy spun wildly, trying to find some angle to penetrate her indifferent exterior. Something, just one thing to impress her.

"And I'm gonna write you into my next book!" I shouted. *Wait, what? Whoa, whoa, whoa, let's not write a check we can't cash.*

"Really?" she said, folding my hair in foil. "You'll have a chapter on hair, or something?"

"Yeah, I already started one about my past hairstylists, so now I have to include you!" I laughed awkwardly, almost skittish, making it all up as I went along. *But why stop there?* Carol inquired. *Why not offer the person you just met an hour ago a treasured family heirloom? Or a kidney?*

"Let me know when it comes out so I can read it," she said, smiling. Her tone was pleasant, she played along nicely. Not rude, just indifferent. Even a cameo in my book couldn't shake this woman loose. I was spent, Tammy had nothing left. We sat in a gentle silence while she finished up. After the highlights set and my hair was rinsed and conditioned, she went about styling my hair beautifully. It had height on the crown yet fell perfectly to my shoulders. The color was lovely—fashionable without trying too hard. I was genuinely blown away—Gina had nothing on her.

"It looks really good, Melanie. I love it," I said, turning to meet her eyes. She smiled and patted my shoulder.

"Good," she said. "I'm glad you like it."

I looked in the mirror, delighted. A curly-hair specialist, more precious than silver. I tucked a curl behind my ear. She took off the smock, I gathered my things, and I followed her to the front desk.

"Wow, your hair!" the girl behind the counter squealed. "Do you love it?"

"I do," I said, catching myself in the mirror behind her. "I'm impressed." I slid my card across the counter and waited, quietly admiring my reflection.

CHAPTER 12
Little Red Bird

I was in my kitchen eating peanut butter with a spoon when I heard a loud bang. It sounded like someone threw a softball at my kitchen window, but that would have been too weird. I went out to my deck, and below the window was a little red bird. Not a bright red, more like a shabby reddish brown. Her left wing was spread out, and she looked so peaceful and beautiful lying there. Not like those regal, brightly colored ones you'd see on the cover of a bird-watcher magazine. She was one of those chirpy, scrappy little birds. They swoop in, take a nibble from your bird feeder, then fly away, busy, busy, busy.

"Oh no," I whispered when I saw her. My lip quivered, "Sweet little bird, I'm so sorry." I don't typically get verklempt over the deaths of wild animals, like birds or squirrels or frogs—and don't even get me started on opossums. So, I was surprised at my emotion and a bit embarrassed.

Rob wasn't home, and I didn't want to leave her on our deck. After too much deliberation, I made the brave choice to scoop her up and remove her. I hoped maybe there was a chance she had a little birdie concussion. That after a spell, she'd rouse her little birdie head, shake it loose, and toddle a few steps before taking flight. Flying free, as little red birdies do.

But I get a little squirrely around dead things and didn't want to touch her, even with gloves. I went into my garage to find a scoop of some sort and found a stiff piece of cardboard. I used it to lift her little body off the ground and carried her to a garbage can at the side of our house, gently placing her on a flattened LaCroix box. I made sure nothing was on top of her in case my concussion hypothesis had some legs.

My daughters, Lucy and Poppy, greeted me as I walked back into the house, curious about what I'd been doing outside with a piece of cardboard and a little red bird. I told them she had bonked her head is all, and that seemed to satisfy them well enough. As they got back to coloring pictures, I cleaned up my kitchen and scooped away a pile of spilled dried oregano on my counter. My mind began to wander to my friend Cindy. It was a random thought, maybe it was because the oregano reminded me of her tobacco, but I was thinking about the way she'd roll her own cigarettes. She was fast and efficient, licking and rolling and smoking them down before moving on to the next thing.

My thoughts meandered to the day she rolled me one. I didn't know it at the time, but our friendship would shift that day and would never be the same. She pulled a small bag of tobacco out of her backpack, then rustled around for her tin of rolling papers. Once she found it, she slipped out a paper, sprinkled a little tobacco in, licked the edge, rolled it, and held it out to me. "Want one?"

Not really, but I'm the kind of person who takes flyers from strangers handing them out on street corners. Not because I'm interested, I don't even look at it. But I can't resist a free gift, so I allow myself to be a middleman between their flyer and the nearest trash can.

So, when Cindy offered me her hard-core, unfiltered cigarette, I accepted her offering and put it to my lips. She flicked her lighter as I leaned in, puffing until the paper came alive. At the time, I only dabbled in social smoking. It was something I did with certain friends, usually with a drink in hand. And they were always "lights," filtered and not something a cowboy would smoke in a Dodge City saloon. Cindy and I had been studying together and had about ten minutes before class. She had a little smoking spot she'd go to, so I followed her there, sometimes running a bit to keep up with her swift little legs. We found a shaded spot and sat down.

Cindy and I were in a master's degree program and had

a similar class schedule. I loved her with my whole heart, but I'm not sure she loved me back in equal measure. Most of us in the master's program were in our early to late twenties, and Cindy was the oldest among us, somewhere in her midforties. She was a single mom, working as a server at an upscale restaurant. Her son was in high school, but I only saw him a handful of times. When I'd go to her house to study, he'd stay in his room, listening to music, coming out for snacks every so often, never acknowledging me at his kitchen table until forced to. "Say hello to Anna," Cindy would say sternly.

"Hi," he'd mutter, grabbing a Coke out of the fridge.

I don't remember if Cindy ever told me what she wanted to do with the second half of her life, why she was getting her master's degree, or what she was doing in Chico in the first place. It was almost as if she were trying on shoes, walking around in them for a year or so to see if they were the right fit, before ultimately deciding that they did, in fact, rub the back of her heels raw.

In master's or PhD programs, the club is more exclusive, and access to professors becomes more intimate. You can no longer hide behind hundreds of other students; you are mentored directly under your professors. It makes it easy for them to seem like gods. Some good, some bad, but all powerful. Not to Cindy, though. She didn't give a crap. And if she didn't like something, she told you about it. Her fierce and gritty independence drew me in. And I felt safer and less vulnerable knowing her.

During one study session at Cindy's house, she was busy making us huevos rancheros. I watched her fondly, thinking that if I ever married an abusive man and retaliated by clubbing him over the head with a candlestick, she'd not only help bury the body, but she'd also handle the logistics. Annoyed by my fits of panic, she'd take over, encouraging me to go home and take a bath just to get me out of her hair. She'd then get back to digging, stopping only to wipe her sweaty brow. And I'm certain we'd get away with it too; the smartest woman in the room would make sure of it.

As she placed a James Beard–level breakfast in front of me, I realized that little spunky woman, with her short, shabby red hair and thick gray roots, was a temporary haven. A home away from home.

The more we studied and attended classes together, the more I noticed her natural intelligence. I often struggled in my courses, studying incredibly hard to get good grades. Yet Cindy was usually smoking, jetting around to and fro, always a busybody, cooking, cleaning up, and fussing about as if she were running late to a destination that didn't exist. Then she'd just zip into class, sit down, and ace everything set before her. It was all too easy, almost beneath her. And I could tell she didn't respect it. I, on the other hand, not only respected it but wanted to leave my mark on academia. I charmed my teachers, whom I greatly admired, sitting studiously in my chair, wide eyed, set on achieving big dreams. She never verbally crushed my fantasy, but her body language told me she'd seen it all, and kid, this don't mean nothing.

There was this one day we studied for a test together at her kitchen table, nibbling on chocolate-covered espresso beans she'd set out for us. I saw her undergraduate diploma on a small bookcase and noticed she graduated summa cum laude. "Are you serious?" I asked, with chocolate covering my teeth. "You randomly decide to go to college at forty and then graduate summa cum laude? Like, it's nothing?"

"Well, it's not exactly rocket science, is it?" she said, rolling another cigarette. I mean, I guess not, but geez.

I could sense Cindy was getting restless. From then on, every time we got together to study, all she did was complain about our professors. Too mean, too dumb, too full of themselves. Our assignments, pointless and useless exercises that took up too much of her valuable time. The shoes were giving her blisters, the politics and arrogance of higher learning an unbearable sting. She opened her sliding glass door, letting in an oppressive haze of Northern California heat. "Man, it's hot," she said, putting her cigarette to her lips. She inhaled deeply before blowing smoke through the screen door. "Makes you wanna . . ." she stopped speaking and paused. I saw her eyes focus on a bird perched on her deck. Her cigarette perched between her fingers, lingering near her lips. "Makes you wanna strip out of your clothes and just fly away . . . free as a bird." She laughed to herself and looked at me. "Know what I mean?"

But I didn't know, not really. I sensed she was getting at something deeper, and I was too young, too sheltered, with too few scars to go there with her. And, in general, I liked to keep my clothes on, even in the oppressive heat. The truth was, I was in my late twenties and life was just beginning to open up for me. And even though Cindy was still so young, just a little bit older than I am now, she seemed like a woman in a hurry. A woman who, for reasons I never understood, feared she was running out of time.

I took a big puff of her rolled cigarette, still a bit wet from when she licked the paper. It bothered me a little, but I tried to be a grown-up about it. This was the first time Cindy ever offered me one, and although I didn't want the dank smell of smoke to follow me into the classroom, I can't say I wasn't curious. I took her cigarette to my lips and inhaled way too deep, launching myself into a coughing fit. "That's straight tobacco, don't hit it so hard," she said, thumping my back. The sky spun, and I was instantly nauseous, taking sips of my bottled water, closing my eyes, willing it to pass. From then on, I'd pretend to smoke until she was finished, buzzing all the while. "Well, shall we go in?" she asked after a few minutes. We squashed the little bit left of our cigarettes under our feet, and I tripped a little following her into the classroom. Cindy was quiet that day, didn't say much. And when class was over, she stood up and smiled faintly, before turning to leave. She walked quickly, she always did, and was gone before I could catch up. I put my notebook into my backpack and headed back to my office.

Things were different after that day. The rigor of our classes gave us a reason to spend time together, but as she began to pull away and show less interest, there wasn't a good excuse for me to come over and eat her huevos rancheros anymore. I shifted and began to bond with other classmates, those closer to my age with a similar commitment to our greater goals. I think Cindy liked me well enough, but she wasn't sentimental. I didn't hold my breath for an invite to stop by for a visit, and I never received one.

As the semester came to a close, students trickled out of the building to go home for Christmas. I spent a lazy afternoon watching TV. Elizabeth Gilbert was a guest on Oprah, celebrating the success of her book *Eat, Pray, Love*. For some reason, I thought of Cindy. Although she never vocalized it, I sensed she was a woman searching for something, trying to go somewhere with nowhere to go. Later that day, on a whim, I went to a local bookstore and bought the book, along with a gift bag and a little card. A week or so later, as I left for the Sacramento airport, I stopped by Cindy's house with my little gift. And tucked inside, a simple card that read,

Cindy,
  Chico doesn't fit you anymore, does it? This book made me think of you. Merry Christmas.
  xx, Anna

I knocked on her door and waited on her stoop, but she never came. The house seemed too quiet for someone to be home, but I didn't want to leave without seeing her, so I knocked again just in case. I stood, my fingers wrapped around the handle of her gift, and waited for five full minutes. I think instinctively I knew I'd never see her again and just couldn't bear to leave. I set the gift against her door and got back in my car. I waited again for one more minute but eventually had to leave to catch a flight back home.

I was in the final year of the program, writing my master's thesis, when a message popped up on my computer. It was from a *C-Kennedy* through AOL Instant Messenger. I jumped and sat back. I hadn't heard from Cindy in two years. After I returned from Christmas break and attended new classes the spring semester, Cindy was noticeably absent. I tried reaching out to her, but I only had her home phone number, and the line would just ring and ring. After a couple of weeks, I asked one of the professors if she was still in the program, and they told me she had withdrawn after Christmas break. Of course, Cindy never bothered to tell me. And not that it matters, but she never called to thank me for my gift either.

"Hi, Anna!" her message read. "You really made a mess of things by giving me that book. I'm in Indonesia, dating a cute little Indonesian man. I'll send you a picture. I'm going to Nepal in a couple weeks. Just wanted to say hi."

My jaw was agape, my eyes crossed. I had so many questions, I didn't know where to start. Like rapid fire, my fingers shot them off, click click click click click click send! I gave her *Eat, Pray, Love* for a little inspiration, a little something to grease the wheels and get her out of the hamster wheel. I didn't think she'd take it literally! And where was her son? How was she paying for this? How is this real life?

I waited a few minutes for a response, but no response came. So, I continued typing anyway, letting her know I was working on my final master's thesis and would be defending it in a few weeks. I told her I was engaged to a man named Rob and that I wouldn't be renewing my contract as a resident director at Chico State for the following year. I told her I missed her and wanted to know more about her life. I missed her huevos rancheros, her rolled-up cigarettes.

Then I waited some more, but she was gone.

That woman really knew how to leave me hanging, and as someone who needs proper closure or struggles in an almost clinical way to move on, she was really starting to tick me off.

As time went on and still no reply, I never got to tell her about graduation, or that my thesis won awards. She never knew I got married and moved back to Omaha, had children, and became a writer. If only she'd just write me back, I could tell her everything. But she was never one to be sentimental, so I didn't hold my breath. Her text, her message, her letter—never came.

A couple of years ago, Cindy was on my mind. She tends to pop up once or twice a year, at random moments, when I'm doing something mundane like rinsing out a cup or trying to find my remote in the couch cushions. She's such a unique woman, I wanted to write about her. The world needed to know about this spunky, fake redhead, and I was dying to know what she was up to. I could write about her adventures in Indonesia and Nepal. Maybe she also went to Naples, like Elizabeth, who knows? Maybe I could write a book all about it, and it, too, would be a bestseller. I started thinking about her story becoming a movie and how much money we could make. I'd get myself a good piece of property, a beautiful little farm. Maybe even my own cow.

I'd call her Nellie and say, "Whoa, Nelly!" every time she gave me grief during a milking. I'd probably get my own chickens. And horses, obviously. My dreams were getting expensive; I needed to find her quick.

So, I did what anyone does when trying to stalk someone—I googled her name. I had to scroll through several different Cynthia Kennedys I knew couldn't be her. Nothing came up, so I tried "Cindy Kennedy Summa Cum Laude Chico CA" and at last, she was a top search result. I even saw a picture of her as a young woman, a teenager maybe? The photo was right above a link to her obituary.

I covered my mouth with my hands. Cindy had died in 2012. In Hawaii, I guess, peacefully in her sleep. She was just fifty years old.

According to the obituary, Cindy did go to Nepal after all. And she must have loved it, because it said she founded the Namaste Children's House orphanage. It was too incredible to imagine. And even though her efforts had nothing to do with me, I was desperate to share a little piece of it. If I hadn't left that book on her front porch, none of this would have happened, right? She wouldn't have been inspired to leave; she wouldn't have made her way to Nepal. I wanted some sort of acknowledgment. Not credit, just something to encourage me that I might have meant something to her. But she wasn't the type. If I had my druthers, she should have at least named her orphanage the Anna Lind Thomas Gave Me a Book That Inspired Me to Create the Namaste House Orphanage. I agree, it's a little long, but still.

Eventually my shock turned into tears, and then into

weeping. It surprised me. Not the crying so much, but the depth of my sadness. The audacity of that woman. She had been dead for years and kept it from me. Swooping in and swooping out before I even realized she's gone.

The next morning after placing the little red bird's body in my trash can, I was anxious to check on her. Our kitchen trash bag was only halfway full, but I needed an excuse. I pulled it out, and all the way through the garage, I prayed I wouldn't see her little body. I prayed she'd just been knocked out and woke up dazed in our trash can, startled and confused. I prayed she regained her strength, flapped her wings, and flew away. As I approached, my heart leaped into my throat when I didn't see her body. She was gone! I ran to the trash can to be sure.

But as I approached, my heart dropped back down again. Her body had slipped behind the LaCroix box. She didn't have just a little birdie concussion; she was dead. And I was silly to imagine it could turn out any other way. I held the trash bag in my right hand, uneasy. Placing it on top of her felt wrong, disrespectful. But after a time, I took a breath and gently placed the trash bag in the can. What else could I do? It wasn't logical to be so sentimental.

The little red bird was dead. And I'm still angry she never said goodbye.

CHAPTER 13
Catherine O'Hara

I was stuck in traffic when I felt it for the first time. My elbow was propped at the window, my face leaning against my hand. *I wonder what shoe size Bea Arthur wore?* I thought to myself. It was then my pinky grazed it. Something firm, soft, and long was stuck to my chin. I tried scraping it, but it sprung right back. I tried pulling it, but it slipped through my fingers. I pulled the sun visor down to see if I could spot it in the mirror, and to my horror, a two-inch-long hair was curled up under my chin. *Is this who I am now?* I wondered out loud. *A woman who has to pluck her thick man hairs?* True, I *am* half Sicilian, but plucking chin hairs is some "Nonna in the old country" nonsense.

Once I broke through traffic, I peeled home and ran toward my tweezers. I ripped the hair out and marveled at the sheer length of it. How could it have grown undetected for so long? I hoped it was an anomaly, some freak accident and not my first step off a slippery slope toward old-lady-ville. But a week later, it was back with a quickness. So quick, in fact, my mirror was like a time-lapse video where I could visibly watch the hair grow and curl under my chin in real time. I've been plucking it weekly ever since. *What's next, a muumuu and a mustache?* I wondered.

I was only in my midthirties, still a mere pup, but my relentless chin hair was a teeny, springy little warning shot that I'm no longer a fresh young woman, and in fact, approaching the first stages of decay. Taking an inventory of my body to plainly inspect its changes was the last thing my psyche needed, but I became desperate for the truth. I discovered some fresh moles that probably needed to get checked, three skin tags on my neck, and pores that looked like you could plant geraniums inside them. But then, oddly, I noticed my nose ring wasn't quite right either. I'd had it for a long time, since my twenty-first birthday. I went to get it pierced with my friend Brady at a cool little tattoo shop in Lincoln, Nebraska. We had gone out drinking the night before once the clock struck midnight, so I warned the piercer that I might bleed a bit more than normal. "The nose really doesn't bleed much," he said. "It's no problem." I was nervous about the pain, so Brady held my hand as the man put the needle through.

"See?" Brady said. "It's nothing, right?" The piercer turned away to grab the stud, and I noticed Brady's eyes grow wide. Then I felt something warm, like water, pouring over my lips.

"What is that?" I asked, sputtering it out of my mouth.

"Sir!" Brady shouted. "Sir, we need you."

The piercer turned around. "Whoa!" He grabbed a white towel and feverishly wiped at my face, and then my chest, blotting it hard on my boobs as if he just spilled red wine all over his mom's favorite rug. I was told to keep my head tilted back, so I could only catch a glimpse of what was going on by the blood-drenched towel rising into view and Brady's disturbed, yet amused eyes. The piercer was in too much of a panic to realize those were actual boobs he was aggressively rubbing with a towel, and at some point, I just needed to call it. "It's fine," I said, grabbing the towel. "I'm fine. Nothing a little stain treater can't fix."

"So sorry, man. I've never seen a nosebleed like that before." He quickly finished the piercing, cleaned off my nose, and showed it to me in a small hand mirror. *Not bad.* The piercing was understated, shimmering in the light just so. I looked good, and I was quite pleased with myself.

"It looks amazing," Brady said as we headed down the busy sidewalk. "Do you love it?"

"I do," I grinned, baring red-stained teeth. "Wanna stop somewhere and get a drink?"

Since I'd only seen myself in a tiny hand mirror, I didn't

realize the impression I must have made on passersby. One woman was walking with her friend and stopped midsentence to stare at me. I thought it was odd. It was just a modest nose ring after all, but some people can be such prudes. It wasn't until I excused myself to the bar bathroom that I realized how wild and deranged I looked. Confronted by a full-length mirror, I looked like Tom Cruise in *Interview with the Vampire* after he sucked the blood out of rats. Dried blood smeared on my lips and chin; my shirt stained red as if I'd been bludgeoned. But the piercing looked so good, I let it slide.

I've had the piercing ever since. But I never expected it to move locations. The piercing itself didn't stretch or get bigger; it moved out of the crease and farther down my nostril. And now that I mention it, it does look longer and now it sometimes smears across my husband's face when we kiss. Everyone in my family has a big, wide nose, and I've always had a thin one. It's a little long, but now it's growing noticeably longer. My Swedish grandpa Henry died when I was a baby, but I've been told I have his nose. A "John Barrymore nose" is what he used to call his. And now I fear mine is turning into more of an "Adrien Brody," so I need it to just take a beat and relax.

For years, I didn't notice the piercing had moved, and now I couldn't see anything else. I hoped getting a loop would make it less obvious, so I made an appointment at a tattoo parlor a block away from my downtown apartment. "Yeah, that'll happen as you age," a man covered head to toe in tattoos said while inserting a new ring in my nose. "As you get older, your nose will continue to grow, moving the piercing even farther."

"So, when I'm sebenty, I'll hab dis weird hoop danging off da tip?" I asked through his gloved hand resting on my mouth.

"Probably not that bad, but it'll move." He clipped the ring and patted my shoulder as a signal I could get up.

Probably not that bad? The cruel hand of time is coming for us all!

Over time, the sting softened, and I tried to remind myself that despite my new witch nose, as well as my ever-growing beard and mustache, there was no need to go into a full-on panic. I was still in my childbearing years, how bad could this be?

Still, a little bad.

One of my most regretful mistakes was googling how old Catherine O'Hara was when she played Kate McCallister in *Home Alone.* I was thirty-seven at the time, lounging on my couch, watching the movie, but mostly scrolling through my phone. My favorite scene is when she lands in Paris, steals the pay phone from an old lady, and hilariously hangs up on the person still chatting on the other line. "Hello? Hello? Hello? Sorry, she'll have to call you back." Gets me every time. It must have been the acting genius of Catherine O'Hara in that scene, because it made me curious about her. *I wonder how old she is in this movie? Early to midforties, maybe?* I'm not sure why I thought she was that age because it wasn't based on her looks. I think it's because *Home Alone* came out when I was an older child, and at that time, Catherine O'Hara was an older mother. To figure it out, I had to do a little math. Google O'Hara's age, google the year *Home Alone* was filmed, subtract, and . . . violà!

Thirty-six.

Wait, wut? Thirty-six? *Uh, no. That can't be right*, I assured myself. I tapped at my phone again, double-checking my numbers.

Thirty-frickity-six.

No, this can't be. My eyes glazed, bewildered. *I'm older than Kevin McCallister's mom?*

It was as if reality took off its white glove and whipped it across my face. My world, tossed upside down. Like a child who finds out they're adopted, or a woman who discovers her husband is living a double life as a clown. My mind fled. *What is real? What is truth? Who am I, what am I doing here, and there's no way I'm older than Kevin McCallister's mom.*

This set off a horrific chain reaction. With urgency, I had to know the age these "older" actresses were when they filmed the movies I loved as a child. "How old was Meg Ryan in *You've Got Mail*?" I typed into the search bar. Apparently, I wasn't the only middle-aged woman curious because once I started typing, it autopopulated right up. The results appeared boldly on my screen. I sat back, shaking my head in disgust. *Wow. So, it's like that, huh?* Meg Ryan was *my current real-life age*, and, in case you're wondering, Tom Hanks was forty. Just a stone's throw away from my tender thirty-seven at the time. Have you seen Tom Hank's neck in that movie? Although handsome and fit, his neck looks like three hot dog buns stacked on top of each other. *Lord, I beg you to have mercy!* I cried inside myself. *I'm the age when necks go bad!*

My existential crisis wasn't because the actresses looked anything less than vibrant and beautiful. It's because I remembered those movies from my childhood, and I saw those women as legitimate adults. Women who owned bookstores. Matriarchs of a wealthy family that flew to France for Christmas. They had teen children named Buzz! There's no way I was old enough for any of that crap.

I'm nearly forty now, and I have all the Tom Hanks neck vibes. I'm noticing new things on my face that I swear weren't there the day before. For me, the first change that caught my eye one lazy Tuesday afternoon was my laugh lines. As I washed my hands in the sink, I looked at myself in the mirror and noticed they had burrowed somehow into deep grooves. Most adults have laugh lines, but mine, seemingly overnight, burrowed deep into grooves so large, one could slide a marble down them for a fun maze game.

It was some time shortly after, I noticed my forehead. I have to say, I don't normally notice my forehead. It's not as if I see a photo of myself and think, *Oh, there's my forehead.* I may notice my thighs and wonder, *Oh dear, is that really what my thighs look like when I'm sitting down?* But I can't think of one time when my forehead caught my eye. Until now.

Only something truly peculiar could cause me to take notice of my forehead. Like a fatty lipoma, a bloody gash, or in my specific case, wrinkles so pronounced it's like I had a pack of hot dogs on my forehead to go with Tom Hanks's neck buns. My mind still refuses to believe this could happen overnight. That just the day before, I had no inkling, no warning, and now I'm at Sephora asking a nineteen-year-old if they sell a primer thick like wall spackle. I needed more time to ease into this.

One of my friends is in her fifties, and at a little get-together, I cornered her to talk about my new forehead. "If I raise my eyebrows, I can hold a quarter in its crease," I said, giving her an illustration. But she wasn't surprised.

"Just wait until you have to put tattoo cover-up on your legs to hide your varicose veins," she said, casual, resigned, taking a sip of her wine. The quarter dropped from my forehead and thumped on the floor. It just never ends. Just this year, I started putting my car's seat warmers on, not because it was cold outside, but to help relax my back. I get charley horses in my neck when I try to pass my child a napkin from the driver's seat. If I don't do a little stretching after a vigorous walk, I wake up the next morning frozen like Stonehenge. I have to squat to pick up a paper clip, and just the other day I was putting on deodorant and saw stretch marks on my armpit. The roller coaster has tipped over the edge, and there's nothing I can do about it now.

My sister, Jenny, is ten years older than me and approaching fifty. She looks incredible, of course, but she's noticed her cycle changing, causing some imbalances and issues. We were setting up the equipment for our YouTube baking show, *Jenny and Anna Bake*, when she told me all about it. "I brought up some of the symptoms I've been having in my Facebook group, and that was a huge mistake," she said, plugging in the light box. "It was just one horror story after another from a bunch of miserable premenopausal women, and I just absolutely refuse to go down like that."

"What kind of stories?" I asked, mincing the garlic. "Hot flashes, weight gain? Stuff like that?"

"Vaginal dryness."

"Vaginal dryness?"

"You heard me."

"So when they walk, it's just a bunch of friction? Kindling catching fire in their pants?" I stopped mincing and cocked my head, concerned.

"Sore, itchy, painful sex, urinary tract infections. It absolutely *will not* happen to me," she said, passing me an onion to chop.

"Well, how can you prevent it?" I asked. I was desperate for any and all knowledge that would help me navigate these pitfalls. "Turmeric? Collagen? Vitamin D?"

"Rebuke it."

"Rebuke it?"

"Yes, I rebuke it in the name of Jesus."

"You're rebuking vaginal dryness in the name of Jesus?"

"Yes, I am, every morning in my prayer closet." She pulled out her Dutch oven and put it on the stove.

"Wait," I said, setting down my chef's knife. "Every morning, you wake up, go into a closet, shut the door, and rebuke vaginal dryness?"

"Yes."

"Like it's the devil?"

"It is the devil."

"What closet are you in?"

"My closet."

"The small one where you keep your toiletries or the large walk-in?" If I was going to be forced to envision this, I needed it to be accurate.

"The walk-in. Think I should go in the small one?"

"I've never rebuked vaginal dryness," I said, moving on to the onion, "so I have no idea. I suppose the most important thing is that you feel comfortable."

"Well, whatever. It's not a closet anyway, it's a war room. I'm releasing strongholds." She began to portion out flour for our bread recipe. I drew within myself, pensive, trying to ingest what my sister was telling me. She's an incredibly funny woman, but she wasn't laughing. "Did you want to start the show with how to make the buns, or what were you thinking?" she asked.

"I'm sorry, wait." I wasn't ready to just move on to bun baking. "So, when you're in the closet, are you shouting, out loud, 'I rebuke vaginal dryness in the name of Jesus!' or what's actually happening? I need to understand."

"I'm not sure how I could make this more clear, but yes. Among a few other things. I declare God's best over my life and the life of my family. Including my health. I pray for my kids, and their lives, their health."

"Can they hear you rebuking vaginal dryness in your closet?"

"I don't know, and I don't care."

I had to admit, her resolve and total lack of embarrassment over the whole thing was inspiring. I've never known anyone fight against vaginal dryness with such tenacity. In fact, I'm sure for a lot of women suffering from vaginal dryness, they fight their battle in the Walgreens lady parts aisle. A closet isn't even crossing their mind.

I walked by a Little League game going on at a field in my neighborhood. I watched the tiny girls, just barely knowing what they were doing in their cute little jerseys, running around bases to the encouragement of their parents and coaches. As I watched, out of the blue I said out loud, "God, I need your help." I had asked him before, but I don't think I really meant it. I didn't really believe I'd *need* help. I had all the tools at my fingertips to get the job done. More books, more information, more education than was necessary to do what was good and right. All I needed was good habits. Expensive supplements. Discipline. And the will to just—do it.

But, for some reason, I wasn't doing it. I hadn't really ever done it. Worse, I didn't believe I could do it. So as parents in their quad chairs hooped and hollered, I asked God for help. A bolt of lightning didn't snap from the sky. Bushes didn't light on fire and start giving me instructions. Nothing happened, really. I took the long way home and walked slow.

The shift was so subtle, I didn't notice it at first. The first weird thing I did was stay up until 4:00 a.m. watching documentaries about women marathon runners. I'm not even sure how I ended up there; I was just scrolling and swiping and then "click"—there I was. I watched in awe as women ran for twenty-one, fifty, a hundred, two hundred miles. Throughout the night, hallucinating, falling, crying, laughing, and stopping occasionally to eat cheese quesadillas. Bloodied feet, lost toenails. Never stopping. Going, going, going.

Their bodies accomplished the impossible because the women asked them to. And then when they were done running, their bodies healed themselves. Incredible. I'd watch one, after another, after another. But why? I never bothered to ask myself.

Then, about a week later, on a whim, I googled local trails and actually read the tedious reviews. As an aside, SuzB needs to calm down with that one-star review because she "couldn't find it." It's not the trail's fault you're stupid!

Before long, I found myself googling "dogs that are good running companions" and spent nearly an hour comparing breeds. After that, I was on a website looking at tiny little weapons I could hide in my pocket, or even wear on my fingers like rings, so I could, I guess, swipe rapey guys in the face if need be. You can never be too prepared. For what, though, I still wasn't sure.

"You know," I said to Rob, looking up from my phone, "I'd really love a German shepherd, but their shedding situation is *soooo* sad."

"Why a German shepherd?" he asked.

"They're handsome. Good family dogs. Good protectors. Good runners."

"Good runners?" he asked. "Why does that matter?" But I still wasn't sure how to answer.

A week after that, I was in the checkout line at Whole Foods and stopped to gaze at the cover of *Women's Running* magazine. As I waited, I pulled it out and flipped through the pages. I think at this point my spirit was tired of dropping hints. *If you don't get it by now, you ain't never gonna get it.* Then, ding! I woke up. "I want to go run."

"What's that?" the cashier asked.

"Oh, nothing. How much is this magazine?"

"Fifteen dollars."

"Good grief, never mind." I put the magazine back.

On its face, the inner call to run is ridiculous. I don't

have the body of an athlete; I have the body of someone who appreciates good wine and soft cheese. I have big boobs and won't even commit to running from a mouse unless I've got on two sports bras. I walk slow. I run slower. My ankle rolls off curbs. I don't sweat, I just puff up and get red. Every time I even try to run, I have to go back home and poop. In other words, there was no logical reason I should run. But my spirit wouldn't leave me alone.

And unlike my half-marathon in Vegas, I knew I wasn't running away from what I had to leave behind. I needed to run toward something waiting for me. But I still didn't fully understand.

I started my run nice and slow and instantly felt it in my lower calves. The burn was concerning, but I also knew my body was like, "What in the world is going on here?" and needed a minute to realize I was serious. I felt the bounce of my body, my hips, my thighs, even my skin. I didn't love it, and it finally occurred to me why people who have no business wearing spandex, like to wear spandex. Sometimes you gotta keep it tight!

I reminded myself to drop my shoulders, to keep my hands loose, to roll through instead of pound. I could hear my breath bounce to the cadence of my feet, and I promised myself I wouldn't stop until the twenty minutes were over. Another runner came at me from the opposite direction. He smiled and waved, as did I, but his pleasantry hit me weird. I felt like crying. And the more choked up I got, the harder it was to breathe. That's an unpleasant sensation, so I shook it off best I could with a little shimmy.

As I trotted along, I gazed at the beautiful lake near the trail. I was getting sentimental now, thanking God for the beautiful world he created, and as I was doing so, I had to roll to a stop as the trail entered the forest. There was a doe standing in the middle of the path. Her head lifted, her ears sticking straight up, and she looked right at me. "Boop, boop, boop!" I yelled, "Go on now, go on." I wasn't scared of her per se, but I was worried that if I tried to get too close, she'd have a sudden freak-out and trample all over me with her long, hoofy legs. "Boop, boop, boop!" I shouted again. I'm not sure why I said "Boop!" instead of something more aggressive, like "Heeya!" but that's all I could think to say at the time.

Still, she wouldn't move. I walked slowly toward her until I was about three arm lengths away. We looked at each other, then just like that, she leaped into the forest. I stood for a moment in disbelief, then, out of nowhere, my lower lip trembled again. I heard a woman say, "On your left!" before speeding by me on her bike. I cleared my throat, desperate to not bring attention to myself, and picked my run back up, navigating the whole weep-while-running fiasco I had gotten myself into. My feet hit the ground, tap tap tap. My breath moving in unison, huff huff huff. And as I emerged from the forested part of the trail, back into the sunlight, I finally understood.

My body wants my respect.

Not some corny meme, not some platitude or body positivity cliché. My body wanted, deserved, and was now demanding my respect. It was turning forty, it's grown now. No more childish, petty games. Enough is enough. *Treat me right.*

I don't think I've ever loved my body, respected my body, or even thanked my body. In fact, I've disrespected it my entire life. And the saddest part is that my body is a miracle. My eyes are a miracle. My hands, my feet. My heart. It pumps every single second—*so I can pursue a joyful life.* It works tirelessly so my spirit can live on earth. Have a family. Have fun. It seals my paper cuts, it fights the flu. It swells to protect an injury. Here I've neglected it, and still, it takes care of me. Yet all I see are laugh lines. Crepey knees. Hot dogs on my forehead. All I see is one curly hair on my chin and ignore the abundance of curly hair it creates for me on my head.

My body wants my respect. To take care of it. To show it love. To be thankful for all it can do. To exercise. To give it sun. And in my specific case, to run. And the only explanation I can figure out, the reason I felt a constant need to cry—is that I was ready to make it right. Running in the midst of answered prayer.

"I'm being way too corny, aren't I?" I asked my mom on the drive home. "Am I overspiritualizing this? A little too woo-woo? Maybe I'm just tired and worn out. Overdramatizing the whole thing."

"Oh no," she said. "It sounds about right to me."

"I want to treat myself well. And then, more than anything, Mom, I want to be content." I turned into my neighborhood. "I want my forties to be my best decade yet."

"It was for me," she said, sipping her tea. "I felt my most

beautiful in my forties. It was when I fully came alive. But my fifties were incredible too. I loved my sixties. My seventies I want to fill with travel. My hip is bothering me a little now, but I'm working on it."

I can remember my mom in her forties. It was when I was ten to nineteen years old. It feels like it was just a week ago, and I don't remember her any different than she is now. My beautiful, Sicilian mother wearing her white boatneck shirts. Black, cropped slacks. Her lovely olive skin. Big brown eyes, a little red mole on her cheekbone. Mom has never worn a lot of makeup; she doesn't have to. I was so proud when she'd come around when my friends would visit after school. When she'd take me to lunch in college and I'd introduce her to all my new friends. I came from that woman. I am a part of that woman. I am that woman.

Catherine O'Hara. Meg Ryan. My mother. And me.

Never stopping. Going, going, going.

CHAPTER 14
Drive

I walked out of the hotel into the Los Angeles sun. I felt a strong urge to throw my beret into the air like Mary Tyler Moore, but I wasn't wearing a beret, and I'd never be caught dead in one. *I really am gonna make it after all*, I thought. I felt it in my bones.

I walked toward a black Cadillac sedan parked in front of the hotel lobby. The driver was an older man and reminded me of a sweet grandpa. He stood by the car, his hands folded in front of him. The two drivers before him were serious and looked like Secret Service agents. One picked me up from LAX holding a large sign with my name on it. As I walked up to him, everyone stared at me intently, thinking I might be a little bit famous, but not real famous, more like someone slated for season twenty of *The Masked Singer* or something. *Have people in LA never seen a celebrity before?* I wondered.

Of course, I'm not famous, but that didn't stop me from enjoying the moment while feeling a sense of loss over my privacy. *Now I know how Lady Gaga feels.*

The second driver picked me up to get a COVID-19 test. The show had me quarantine in my hotel for two full days, and on the second day, I was driven to the Universal Studios lot, where my driver made his way into a parking garage. He rolled down my window for a woman in a hazmat space suit. "What show?" she asked. The driver spoke for me, then she looked at me, "Your name?"

"Anna Thomas," I said. She searched, flipping the top page back and forth. "Maybe it's under Anna *Lind* Thomas?" and at that she found me. *I bet that never happens to Gaga either,* I thought. People tend to get a little confused with my name. I often hear, "Is Lind a part of your last name or is it a part of your first name, like Mary Lou?"

It's just my maiden name that I use more as a middle name for professional purposes, and I can see now that I've made it really complicated for people who need to find me on a list.

The woman in the space suit swabbed my nose, and

after a few pleasantries, we slowly drove away from the parking garage. My eyes could barely take it all in. We must have been near *The Ellen DeGeneres Show* studio because there were pictures of her everywhere, three stories tall. As we exited the lot, I was captivated by all the midcentury, extremely ill-kept tiny homes butted up against each other surrounding the immediate area. Back in the days of old Hollywood, I bet these were gorgeous, coveted little homes, but now most of them were dumps. As if years ago, someone in the industry left under the cover of darkness, and a squatter moved in to relax and smoke his crack in peace. They were probably rentals now, and tenants must be paying gazillions per month. *Can the owners not afford a paint job with a small portion of those gazillions?* My curiosity about it still haunts me.

But on this day, the day of my shoot, I was picked up by a grandpa who offered me some candy.

"So, we're headed to Jim Henson studios?" he asked, looking at me through his rearview mirror.

"That's what the email told me!" I said with more enthusiasm than the conversation called for. I cleared my throat and looked out the window.

"So, what do you do then?" he asked. I was surprised he was so chatty since the other two, while very polite, barely said a word on our drives.

"I'm a writer," I told him.

"Oh *really*?" he said, turning on his blinker. "I've been doing this awhile and I thought for sure you were a model. Or maybe an actress, *but a writer*?" He seemed shocked, and as we met eyes in his rearview mirror, I raised my eyebrows in surprise, but I was also quite pleased. I've told countless people I'm a writer, and no one has ever been shocked. In fact, for many, it seems to explain why every time they see me in public spaces, I'm in loose loungewear with a ranch dressing stain on my thigh.

I looked out the window to the bright California sun and felt a warm peace wash over me. In Nebraska, I'm a frumpy writer. But in California, I'm a model. Or maybe an actress. *Who knew?*

"So, are you a screenwriter, or . . . ?" Grandpa Driver asked.

"No, I'm a book author," I said. I could tell it was a little confusing, so I tried to clear it up. "I'm here because a funny story I wrote years ago went viral and I've been cast to tell the story to celebrity hosts." I could tell Grandpa Driver didn't fully get it, and quite frankly, neither did I. We let it be.

As we pulled into the studio, a tall, large woman in a security outfit giving off vibes she could handle her own stopped us at the gate.

"Hi there," Grandpa Driver said. "I'm dropping off Anna Thomas." The woman flipped through papers on her clipboard, back and forth, scanning. "It's probably under Anna *Lind* Thomas," I shouted from the back seat. And at that, she found me.

"I'm trying to figure out what you're doing out here, standing in the hot sun?" Grandpa Driver asked the security woman. "You look like you should be inside, starring in these movies," he said, waving his hand. The woman coyly smiled as butterflies emerged and fluttered around her head. "Oh stop," she said, slapping his arm, "you can go through."

My relaxed, easygoing, "this feels like destiny" demeanor turned a bit more rigid and suspicious after witnessing his banter with another woman. *Oh, I see,* I internally spat. *I guess these compliments are a dime a dozen.*

He gently pulled up to a tent where I had to be COVID-19 tested again before entering. He got out and opened my door. "I'll be the driver who picks you up," he said softly, smiling sweetly. "You knock 'em dead, kid." He winked and it felt familiar. I had been all alone, but not anymore.

"I will," I said as a young woman in a space suit aggressively swabbed my nose. "I promise, I'll make you proud."

"I already am," he said, raising his hat.

And for some reason, I believed him.

I found myself out of place, wandering through the Jim Henson studio lot with a suitcase big enough to comfortably transport Danny DeVito. As time went on, I worried my suitcase was leaving a bad first impression. When I started packing for my trip to Los Angeles, it was obvious I was in dire need of a suitcase upgrade. I ended up using my husband's, because mine was fifteen years old and the handle no longer extended all the way. It's not like Rob's suitcase was any better. He bought it for our honeymoon twelve years ago, and both of ours look like suitcases that fell out of a car and were driven over by a semitruck.

As I pulled his off a high shelf in our storage room, it was hard to miss the thick layer of dust and cobwebs from lack of use. Since having babies, Rob and I haven't gone anywhere or done anything. Family trips are too exhausting with small children and induce the same survival stress hormones experienced by someone whose ship is about to capsize. The only difference is, you're not holding your crying children on the *Titanic* while anxiously waiting for a small boat; you're at Disney World waiting for a teacup.

Technically, I didn't need such a large suitcase. I was told to bring only a couple outfits the stylists had chosen earlier. But since I was responsible for my own clothes, I wasn't taking any chances. It takes great courage to wear your own clothes on national TV as a mother of young children, and I wasn't the least bit prepared. I could still feel the chill that shot through my body as I read the email from the production assistant.

> Hi, Anna! Please try on five to six full outfits, with shoes, and send us head-to-toe photos for our stylists by Friday. Think smart casual, but we want you to be you!

I froze. It never occurred to me that I'd be responsible for my own "style." I wasn't sure *who* would be responsible for my style, exactly, but I suspect I subconsciously envisioned my moment on national TV as an opportunity to be transformed into someone completely different: sloppy mom in house robe with frizzy hair in high bun spends two hours with Carson Kressley and emerges on stage in fitted skinny jeans she never would have been caught dead in before. "But you know what? I love it!" With a loud floral button-up, perfectly fitted to make room for her melon boobs. "I've never considered wearing fuchsia flowers, but you know what? I love it!"

But no, I was left all alone with my own pathetic closet with nary a good-looking, stylish gay man to help me.

If you force me to describe my "style" after a full year of COVID-19 restrictions, I'd probably call it "elevated lounge-wear." And the only reason it was "elevated" is because I started to get depressed in my "lowered loungewear" and went on a rebellious shopping spree at Athleta that I'm still making payments on. What's worse, a month prior I had KonMari'd my entire closet with fervor. KonMari is the Japanese name for the famous organizing consultant Marie Kondo, known for her controversial KonMari Method of only keeping items in your home that you *love* and bring you *joy*, and tossing the rest. It's easy to do. Ask yourself, "Do I love it?" and if the answer's no, toss it. When you're done, your house will look naked and sad as if it's been foreclosed. Success!

The year 2020 made me acutely aware of my home and all the things I didn't like about it. My closet is a small, narrow walk-in, and the amount of clothes I had hanging up and folded on shelves made me feel as if I were step-ping into thick Amazonian brush every time I got dressed in the morning. I'm not clinically claustrophobic, but I have tendencies, which is why I hate my closet. And tiny elec-tric cars.

Something had to be done. To pump myself up, I binged on Netflix's *Tidying Up with Marie Kondo* and followed up with a shot of her book, *The Life-Changing Magic of Tidying Up*. I threw my entire closet of clothes onto my bed and started shoving them into large black garbage bags as if I'd just committed a crime and had to skip town. I was methodi-cal, steely, emotionless. Some clothes were easy to get rid of. If I hadn't worn it for a decade, it could go. But there were a lot of clothes I tossed simply because they were worn most often by "Ten Pounds Heavier Anna." What I failed to consider, however, was those clothes also gave me great comfort after a large meal, during my period, or on days I craved the sweet tenderness of worn-out elastic. And now, thanks to KonMari, they were gone.

After I cleared my bed, I had four large bags of clothes that were so heavy, I could only push them across the floor. My closet looked like a barren wasteland. It only held some V-neck T-shirts, a variety of tank tops, some nice blouses, a few casual dresses, a handful of cardigans, and two blazers worn by "Ten Pounds Heavier Anna" but were so expensive I couldn't part with them. I'm confident Marie would have gently encouraged me to let them go, but that's too bad.

The clothes I kept in bags were in good shape, and most were name brand. In hopes I could make a little side change, I decided to swing by the Just Like New! consignment store for an exchange. I pushed my black bags toward the car, dragging and rolling and tearing up the sides on the rough surface of the driveway. Rob was at work, but it didn't stop me from resenting him. *I didn't get married so I'd have to carry heavy things!* I muttered. Of course, I could have just waited until he got home, but the KonMari Method waits for no man.

Once I got to my SUV's trunk, I had to pump myself up, like I was in a Strongman competition faced with a boulder. After a few rounds of deep, rapid breaths, similar to Lamaze, I picked up the first bag and got it to my knee. I Lamazed again, then hoisted it into the trunk, grunting and sweating, trying to do a crouch maneuver because that's what middle-aged people do to protect their back.

I pulled up to Just Like New! and sighed heavily as I faced the immense labor before me. What had started out as grit and determination morphed into frustration and resentment. Heavy things can really wear a person down, testing their resolve with every pulled muscle. I decided the best plan of attack was to get it over with, dragging the bags two at a time, one in each hand. After plopping them out of my trunk, I grabbed the bags and lunged forward, digging my Nike slides into the pavement. After gaining some momentum, I harnessed it to make my way across the parking lot, into the store, and to the counter, where a bored teenage girl, now annoyed she'd have to rummage through yet another person's crap, gave me a ticket. "I have two more after this," I said, breathless. Clearly put off, she meandered away from the counter.

I was sweating now, full-on pitting out, humiliated. As I grabbed my other two bags from the trunk, I couldn't quite put my finger on why I felt embarrassed. Did the whole thing whiff of desperation? Was the amount of labor I was willing to suffer in exchange for pocket change too pitiful? I activated my quads and really dug in, getting to the door faster this time, but my large bags got stuck in the doorway. Completely over it, I gave the bags one huge yank, ripping them both at the sides as clothes spilled out. Supported by zingy and resentful stress hormones, I scooped up my clothes and tossed them behind the counter. "Here!" I said to the back of the teenager's head. "Throw 'em in the trash for all I care!"

She turned, "Um, we don't throw unwanted items away; that's your responsibility. Ma'am? Ma'am!"

"Just call me when you're done!" I shouted over my shoulder and speed walked back to my car. I sat in the driver's seat for a while, regaining my breath and composure. I have an easygoing personality, and it takes quite a bit to light my fuse, but once it catches fire, I can blow at any minute. I made my way out of the parking lot and was nearly home when I received an automated phone call. "We've reviewed your items, please return to Just Like New!" The message filled me with dread as if I were on trial and the jury returned with a verdict a little *too quickly*. I made a U-turn back to the store.

"Yeah, we decided not to keep any of the items. Here's your clothes back," the smug teenager said, pointing to my clothes near the doorway that were now consolidated into two gigantic bags, each the size of a Volkswagen Beetle.

As a God-fearing woman who'd rather not go viral for making a scene, I buried the stresses of the previous few hours down deep. With a gritty staccato pattern, I replied, "Oh. Really? I'm surprised. Some of those are American Eagle. And still have the tags on them."

"Right. We only buy clothes lightly used that are up to date with the latest trends and fashion," she said, curling her cheeks into a fake smile. "Thanks though." I looked behind me and saw a woman with a short perm holding a dress up to her body that looked hand sewn by a Quaker. I turned and smiled weakly before saying, "Makes sense."

I grabbed both bags, not caring if my arms popped out like a Mrs. Potato Head, and let my rage-induced adrenaline help me thrust the bags in my trunk. At a nearby Walgreens, I remembered seeing a Salvation Army drop-off container, so I put my car in drive and made my way there.

The only problem was, the opening into the container was about five foot high, and I'd have to lift each bag over my head to get it inside. I'd gone too far and suffered too much to give up—it was time to finish this. I went back to my Lamaze breathing, hoisted the bag to my knee, and then after two deep breaths, I lifted the bag high over my head. As I tried to pull my arms forward to throw the bag inside the container, I felt my body tipping backward. It's embarrassing to fall in public, but it's extra embarrassing to fall so slowly you could make eye contact with someone and say, "Sorry to bother you, but could you lend me a hand?" while it's happening. Eventually, with the bag still over my head, my back smacked the pavement as clothes spilled all over the Walgreens parking lot. When I discovered tiny parking lot pebbles were buried deep into my butt cheeks, I felt my only option was to foam at the mouth and throw all the clothes into the container piece by piece, maniacally, until that hellscape of an afternoon was over. Shoppers leaving Walgreens all watched in horror, some holding their purses, and children, tight to their bodies.

But eventually, it was finished. Every single item of clothing I didn't love, like, or wear was now gone.

And this was nice, for about a month or so, until a production assistant asked me to go into my bare closet, pick out five to six outfits, including shoes, for my appearance on a TV show. On a major network. I think they assumed I, along with the other cast members, would have clothes we actually liked in our closets. They were wrong. I realize the whole point of KonMari is to love what you keep, but that theory goes right out the window when you're asked to pull something out of it for national TV. As far as I was concerned, it was all garbage. Light it on fire! I was left with no other option than to grab my purse, head to an outlet mall, and go into credit card debt. I fired up my car and prayed for a miracle.

The Jim Henson studio lot was charming, like you stepped into another time, another world. It used to be Charlie Chaplin's studio and dripped with history. You could feel it. Certain areas had cobblestoned paths, making my large rolling suitcase loud and obnoxious as I strolled around looking for some sort of signage, or a person to tell me where to go. Fortunately, I was pleased with the outfits in my suitcase, thanks to a satisfactory selection at J.Crew Factory. Unfortunately, I naively assumed I'd lose twenty pounds before the shoot and bought my knit blazers two sizes too small. There has to be a life lesson in there somewhere—how I can't ever accept the way I currently am and assume, with confidence, future me will be far better—more disciplined, fit, and glamorous. Then the day of supposed transformation arrives, and I look in the mirror. I'm just me, the way I've always been, except now I'm wearing a blazer two sizes too small and it shows.

After just enough wandering and clickity-clacking to feel self-conscious, I ran into people who looked at me with recognition. Some were producers, and even though their mouths hid behind masks, I saw smiles in their eyes. "Are you Anna?" they asked. We bumped elbows and I met the showrunner. She struck me as funny, firm, and in control. I liked her instantly. Everyone I met was cool and warm, and the showrunner, Macy, brought me to my dressing room. It was large and spacious and made me feel like I was someone with something important to say. In reality, it was just a story about farting on a date, but after 2020 I felt a clear resolve: America desperately needed a good old-fashioned fart story.

As I laid out my suitcase, the stylist came into my room as if she were a surgeon about to remove my appendix. She wore a bright blue surgical gown, with a mask and visor. However, I sensed a super cute outfit with impeccable hair and makeup underneath. Out of all the styles I sent them with the J.Crew Factory tags still on, they chose a knit camel blazer (two sizes too small) with a black V-neck and black pants ensemble. Thanks to Pinterest, I knew that was "on trend."

I got dressed, stylist approved, and she sent in hair and makeup. I noticed I wasn't nervous, and it felt odd. That morning, in my hotel room, I had prayed. I prayed I wouldn't be nervous. I was so weirdly alone, I prayed he'd simply be with me, so I could feel his presence. Even though I knew I'd soon be sitting across from two celebrities, I didn't want to put anyone on a pedestal. I wasn't there to impress anyone, to get them to like me. I wasn't there to perform like a monkey in front of other people or secretly hope they'd be so awed they'd offer me my own show to host next season (although the thought did cross my mind). I chose to trust God to open and close doors. The pressure was off, they couldn't do anything for me, I was free to be me. I asked for the courage to truly believe it. "I just want to make you proud," I said, looking out my hotel window at the Burbank Airport. "And I will. I'll make you so proud."

While I waited in my dressing room to go on stage, I tried to find my pulse. I obviously had one, but where was it? I asked God to help with my nerves, but I worried he might have overdone it with the spiritual Valium. I heard a knock on my door as it opened. "You ready?" the stage manager asked.

And then, I felt it. My heart, beating all along.

I sat across from the celebrity hosts, laughing casually, as one does, over Peppa Pig. We were on a set designed to look like a library study. They wore velvet jackets as we all sat in large velvet chairs, bonding over our children's favorite shows. "I especially love Daddy Pig," I added. "Dude's hilarious." Then I took a swig of water and never felt more alive.

We weren't talking about Peppa Pig during the actual taping, of course; that would be dumb. We were just small talking while the stage director had her crew fix a reflection coming off a fake window behind us.

"Do you have any of the Peppa Pig books?" one of the hosts asked me.

"Pffft, probably all of 'em. You got a favorite?" I shot back another sip of water.

After the crew finished fixing the window, the stage director announced they were done, and we could resume shooting again. On cue, I leaned right back into my fart story. My mind methodically fed my mouth all the lines I needed to say, and it was so precise, I was able to mentally step away and observe what was happening in awe. I didn't fumble, I didn't have to start over. I didn't forget to hit my marks. It was natural and easy, everything I needed it to be. My prayers were being answered in real time. We had to take another quick break while the crew fussed with lighting, and the stylist came up to me and adjusted my shirt. "You're doing so good," she whispered through her mask.

"Do I look okay?" I asked. "Am I sitting up straight, not too hunched over?"

"No, I'm watching you in the monitor," she said, running a lint stick over my boobs. "I'd adjust you if you didn't. You look great." She stepped away as the makeup artist squatted in front of me.

"Hey you, let me touch up your lipstick," she said, wiping my lips with a thin little brush. The makeup artist and I had bonded earlier, laughing in my dressing room just moments before. We shared intimate details of our lives in a way that's only *not weird* in a hair salon. Whenever I'm in a salon or spa, I open right up like it's a counseling session. It just feels so natural to be offering personal insights, like my deep insecurities, or how I'm a lazy lover. I think it's because their services require such close contact. A strange intimacy is exchanged as they wash your hair, rub moisturizer on your cheeks, or smear color on your lips. They tell you every tawdry detail of their divorce; you tell them you haven't had a normal period in six months. It just makes sense somehow.

"Your hands smell good, like citrus," I said.

"That's just part of the job," she laughed.

"Remember when smoking was still a thing," the hairstylist said behind me, while adjusting my hair, "and everyone smoked cigarettes attached to a fork so their hands wouldn't stink?"

"Oh, I remember those days well," the makeup artist said, putting the lipstick back in her bag. She gathered her things, crouched by my ear, and asked, "Are you killing it?"

I nodded.

"Good."

The hairstylist gave me a few final touches. "Remember," I whispered to her, "the higher the hair, the closer to God."

"You're very close to him," she assured me. The producer made the final announcement, and the hairstylist moved off stage. She turned to look at me with such a big smile behind her mask, her eyes lit right up.

I felt at ease and realized these women—the stylist, the makeup artist, and the hairstylist—were so much more than their titles and their ability to make me look good. For just that moment, they were best friends, confidantes, and cheerleaders. Just by spending those few nerve-racking moments with me before I went on stage, they were now familiar in an unfamiliar setting. They huddled close to me as they fussed all around me, whispering their encouragement. They smiled behind their face masks, made fun of their medical hazmat suits, and let me know they were right off camera. See? Just right over there. If anything goes wrong, they'll fix it. I didn't have to worry if I had lipstick on my teeth, my hair was sticking up, or my jacket crumpled in all the wrong ways. I could simply be in the moment for one of the biggest moments of my life.

I settled back into my chair, and when it was time, we finished the story. The hosts loved it. We laughed together, they were hilarious, it was easy and fun. "That's a wrap!" I heard someone say off stage. It was hard to see with all the bright lights. I turned to the hosts, "It was an honor meeting you," I told them, "truly." I pressed the palms of my hands together in gratitude. We said our goodbyes as Macy emerged to greet me at the stage. I scanned her face to see if she was pleased.

"Anna," she said, as if trying to get my attention across the room, "that-was-*amaaaaaazing*." My tense shoulders melted to my feet. "I'll meet you in your dressing room in a few minutes."

Macy and another producer discussed final notes in my room and went over a few things they wanted to reshoot, like the hosts' opening lines into the segment. I went back on stage, we said a few lines, and then just like that, it was over. I was free to go.

An assistant walked me back to my dressing room, where I collected my things and raided the complimentary snack bar, shoveling granola bars and gummy bears into my suitcase. A production assistant knocked on my door and offered to walk me back to the car. My momentary best friends were outside chatting. We all said our goodbyes, the makeup artist pulled out her phone and followed me on Instagram. I would have hugged them if it was allowed. We waved, instead.

I followed the assistant into the lot and through an alleyway. My giant suitcase clickity-clacked behind me. We turned a corner, and I saw Grandpa Driver waiting by his sedan.

"There she is!" he boomed. "How'd you do?"

I walked right up to him and smiled. "I crushed it."

He grabbed my suitcase and put it in the trunk. "I knew you would, kid," he said, shutting the trunk closed. "I knew you would." He opened the car door and I stepped inside. I opened a fun-sized Twix bar he had in a cup next to me and looked out my window.

"Look, see the Hollywood sign in between those buildings? Pretty cool, huh?" Grandpa Driver said, pointing above him. I ducked my head to see, and there it was. I smiled and sat back, casually observing a man peeing on the sidewalk. I did what I came to do, and it's over now.

Of course, it was just a sliver, a segment, a piece of one episode. Nothing big, nothing crazy. My story was just one of many, and it will air and then slip away like a wisp of smoke. Or maybe, since it's Hollywood, it won't even air at all. But I did it. And all these people, all these strangers, who blew in my life for just a moment, gave me precisely what I needed, right when I needed it. They likely forgot about me already, but I'd never forget them.

I took a bite of Twix and felt a little pang in my chest. I missed my babies and was ready to go home. Grandpa Driver looked at me through the rearview mirror.

"Want me to stop somewhere? Need anything?"

"No," I told him, smiling. "I don't need a thing."

Acknowledgments

To my husband, Rob. Even though I constantly trip over your gigantic shoes, and you clean the kitchen like someone who has just recently gone blind, I'd be miserable without you. Look at all we've made together. Aren't we just so proud?

Mom. Thank you for counseling me when the writing is hard. Thank you for celebrating the work when I get it just right. Thank you for editing my first drafts and stopping every five minutes to call me, sobbing from laughter. It's in those moments, the sobbing, the gasping, the way you can't get a word out and I just sit there like, "What? What is it? What's so funny? Is it the line about Dad falling down the stairs?" when I'm filled to the brim with confidence. I can do anything I set my mind to.

Dad. Thank you for teaching me what it means to have a sense of humor. It's an art, really, the ease at which you laugh at yourself, how you see humor in all things. Never taking yourself, or life, too seriously. All those years laughing together at the kitchen table, or just the two of us huddled together at a party, whispering and guffawing among ourselves. It's made me who I am.

ACKNOWLEDGMENTS

Jenny. My sister, my biggest fan. My best friend. *Jenny and Anna Bake* will be huge someday, and oh! We'll have so much fun!

Christian. My big brother. My protector from bullies. You make a delicious tomato sauce.

Amber Knowles. Remember when I brought you to a book signing as my hype woman and we not only sold out of books, but they had to buy the books we had stashed in the trunk? The little old lady manager came up to me and said, "Every writer needs an Amber," as she patted my hand. It's true. I love you.

Gene Pellegrene. When facing my manuscript's looming deadline, you offered me your swanky artist loft in Chicago for an entire week. Free! I did some of my best writing in that leather chair you have in the guest room. And I ate all your food, man. It was embarrassing. What's worse, you wouldn't let me repay you. So, I promised to put you in my book. Here it is. It's not nearly enough. Thank you.

Erin Niumata. You're not just an agent, but a mentor and friend. And you make me laugh. It doesn't get better than that.

Jenny Baumgartner. You set me free to be the writer I'm meant to be. And with just the smallest comment, side note or critique, can push me to write things I didn't know I had in me. Thank you.

Of course, Jenny wasn't alone—the entire Nelson Books team are wonderful. Thank you, *Kristina Juodenas*, for bringing the vision of my cover to life—I think I like this cover better than the first! To *Stephanie Tresner*, it can't be easy managing the marketing efforts of someone's dream.

You handle it with professionalism, grace, and a good sense of humor. Thank you for helping me make my dreams come true. To publicist *Sara Broun*—who hustled on my behalf and landed me some pretty sweet gigs—thank you. And to editor *Janene MacIvor*, thank you for your steady guidance facing an impossible deadline. You are patient, kind, and very good at what you do.

Lucy and Poppy. My girls. As I'm writing this, you are five and seven years old. Oh, how we laugh and laugh! It's ridiculous how much I look forward to our "Fri-Yay" nights, even though you're both sore losers at UNO. Crying, laughing, winning, losing, laughing, fighting, loving, laughing, all our live long days.

About the Author

Anna Lind Thomas is a humor writer and popular online personality who founded the funny site *HaHas for HooHas*. She spends her time writing for various media outlets and hosting her podcast, *It's Not That Serious*, which consistently ranked in the Top 25 of the iTunes Family section. She holds a bachelor's in advertising and a master's in communication studies and spent many years copywriting and creating campaigns in ad departments before having children. Her story about a fart went viral and catapulted her to fame (or infamy). Anna and her husband, Rob, live in Nebraska with their two young daughters, Lucy and Poppy, and an English Bulldog named Bruno. You can learn more at AnnaLindThomas.com.

She'd love to hang out with you on Facebook.com /AnnaLindThomas or on Instagram.com/Anna.Lind.Thomas. And if you love the book, text her at 402-915-1727. It will make her day. *Seriously.*